Homer Returns
More True Tales of a Blind Wonder
Cat & His Fur Family
Gwen Cooper

Interrobang Books

Copyright © 2023 by Gwen Cooper

All rights reserved.

No portion of this book may be reproduced in any form without written permission from the publisher or author, except as permitted by U.S. copyright law.

Contents

Chosen	3
Getting There is Half the Fun	33
The Infestation	58
Love in a Cold Climate	87
Nothing Bad Ever Happens in Stars Hollow	108
Homer Returns	127
About the Author	148

Chosen

Pandora ("Pandy" for short) was a purebred Siamese and could only be described— although this phrase wasn't in common use twenty years ago—as a hot mess.

Some of her problems were obvious even to a casual observer. For one thing, Pandy was morbidly obese. She had all of a Siamese cat's fine-boned delicacy of frame from the shoulders up and the hips down. But her midsection carried an excess seventeen pounds of pure lard. The tiny, porcelain-doll perfection of her head and neck made for a jarring contrast with the enormous belly—ballooning out on each side of her body—that swayed ponderously as she walked. Watching Pandy stroll about the house always made me think of a song popular on Miami dance radio at the time, which admonished, *Shake it . . . don't break it . . . took your mama nine months to make it...*

I loved Pandy dearly, but I was probably the only one who did, aside from Maggie, my boyfriend Jorge's mother. She didn't do a very good job of keeping her hindquarters clean, bless her heart. (Pandy, that is—not Jorge's mother.) Whether this was because her girth hampered her ability to reach around and *get in there*, or because Pandy had given up in some fundamental way, was unclear. But every upward flick of her tail revealed an incriminating brown ring, as permanently fixed as if it were tattooed to her fur, no matter how often or assiduously Maggie tackled Pandy with the Baby Wipes.

Pandy would unerringly zero in on the visitors and houseguests who were the least interested in cats, and when—after she'd repeatedly pawed at their legs for attention—the hapless visitors would finally relent and try to pet her, she would lash out violently, leaving confusion, claw marks, and little tufts of yellow Siamese fur in her wake as she fled for refuge under Jorge's parents' bed. And woe betide the unsuspecting cat lover who attempted a friendly scritch behind Pandy's ears and ended up pulling back a bloodied hand for their trouble.

At seven years old, Pandy still suckled daily at the long-dry teats of her mother, Persephone (aka "Persy"), from whom she'd never been separated a day in her life. This, according to Maggie, was the true source of what was alternately referred to as "Pandy's quirks," "Pandy's problems," or, perhaps most accurately, "Pandy's neuroses."

"Cats aren't supposed to live with their mothers their whole lives," Maggie would say. And then she'd add, "Nobody is, really."

In human years, Pandy would have been somewhere in her mid-forties. I thought about *Grey Gardens* and *The Glass Menagerie,* and the entire literary pantheon of bitter or dotty middle-aged spinsters who'd never left their parents' homes—and then I tried to imagine what I might be like if I were still living with my own mother when I was in my forties.

"Definitely not," I'd agree, with a shudder.

I was twenty-three and had just moved in with Jorge, my first serious relationship post-college. We were living in a small one-bedroom apartment in a two-story low-rise owned by one of Jorge's uncles, nestled deep in the warren-like side streets of Little Havana. The people living all around us had emigrated from the mountains of Cuba, and they kept chickens in the postage-stamp backyards of their tiny, ranch-style homes. It was an odd (and often irritating) thing to be living in Miami in the 1990s—among bustling traffic and construction and silvery skyscrapers gleaming on the horizon—yet wake up at five thirty every morning to the sound of roosters crowing twenty yards away.

My own family were also "animal people." My father liked to spend time at the stables where Miami's mounted police kept their horses, and the puppies we adopted came from these animal-loving officers, inevitably with some heart-rending back story: Misty, a petite German shepherd/whippet cross, had been thrown from a moving car on I-95; Casey, a yellow pit bull/Lab mutt, had been used as bait in a dog-fighting ring. And so on.

We made much of these dogs, conspicuous even in a neighborhood of pampered, pedigreed pooches as a family who "spoiled their dogs rotten." Often we came home to find that one or another of our neighbors' dogs had escaped from his own yard and was camped out on our front porch. We would joke that the neighborhood dogs must have some kind of communications network, a way of telling each other that while they all might be treated well, at the Coopers' a dog lived like a king! We laughed about it, but I do think we were always trying—with years of love and slavish attention—to make up for those early traumas our dogs had suffered.

I'd always imagined that I would get a dog of my own when I finally moved into my first "grown-up" apartment. But the place Jorge and I shared was very small, without so much as a proper patch of grass for a dog to run and play on—and, as young adults striving to build our careers, the hours Jorge and I worked were long. I was running a youth outreach program that promoted community volunteering among middle- and high-school students. Jorge was a production assistant on commercial video shoots. When we weren't working, we were often at after-hours networking functions, trying to make the connections that would give us the next leg up. Nothing in our lifestyles seemed conducive to canine guardianship.

Still, as far as I was concerned, a home wasn't a home at all if there weren't any animals living in it.

The highlight of my week was always Sunday, when we'd go out to brunch with Jorge's parents and then back to their house to while away the afternoon until Sunday dinner. It was a joy to spend time with Pandy and Persy and Olympia—a slender, auburn-hued Abyssinian—along with the family dog, a coal-black pit bull named Targa. Targa was more utterly gaga over humans than any dog I've known before or since. In fact, Jorge's parents' house had been robbed three times (such was Miami in the '80s and early '90s) while Targa was in it—and, according to the one intruder the police had eventually caught, Targa had done little to foil the burglars beyond licking them ecstatically and bringing over her toys.

Targa may have loved people, but she hated all three cats with a deep and murderous hatred. I never witnessed any of it firsthand, but I heard stories of close calls and surprise attacks that very nearly ended in bloodshed. Jorge's parents never left Targa and the cats together unsupervised when they were out, and even when they were home they always kept Targa's muzzle close at hand.

The feeling was more than mutual. The cats delighted in finding little ways to goad Targa when they thought no one was looking. Pandy, in particular, would take malicious glee in peeing on Targa's dog bed the moment Targa left it unattended to play in the backyard.

As I said, many of Pandy's problems in life were apparent at a first glance. That Pandy was a menace to new people, however—or even to people she already knew; Jorge, his father, and his sisters bore their share of Pandy-inflicted war wounds—was something I didn't know initially. I didn't find out for months, until Maggie confided it to me one afternoon in a kind of shocked undertone, upon finding a blissed-out Pandy, purring and unconscious, draped across my legs. By that point, Pandy and I were already deep into the early stages of our four-year love affair.

Pandy and I fell for each other instantly, from the first day we met.

Jorge's family were a bookish clan, and I was a reader myself. Many a Sunday would find me lounging in one of the comfy chairs in his parents' living room, nose buried in a novel while Pandy sprawled on my lap or my chest, belly fat oozing out and around until her body was an enormous perfect circle atop which perched a teeny-tiny cat's head.

Her weight should have made her an unwieldy lap cat; the body heat generated by her bulk should have made her a sweaty, uncomfortable burden on a humid Miami day. But something about us just meshed, and neither of those things ever bothered me. Pandy's rumbling purr was a deep, intensely happy vibrato that sank into my chest and radiated through my entire body as I absentmindedly stroked her back or rubbed her chin in between turning book pages. If I got too immersed in my novel and neglected to pet her for more than a few minutes, Pandy would bonk her head against my hand or paw gently at my shoulder until petting was resumed. My fingers seemed to know instinctively how to find just the right scratching spots that would make her purr deepen, her half-closed eyes turned to my own in a gaze of such melting adoration that it could break your heart.

As for me, I sometimes felt that I hadn't known true serenity until those Sundays with Jorge's parents, when the late-afternoon sunlight would slant through the windows and transform the fur of Pandy's rising and falling chest, lying across my own, into a gleaming mound of golden flax.

Pandy's instant affection for me—unprecedented in the annals of Jorge's family lore—became something of a tall tale among them, the story about The One Person Pandy Liked. It was heady stuff for a budding, inexperienced ailurophile.

You heard all the time about people who one day discovered some latent talent or ability they'd never known they had. Maybe *I* was one of those people. Maybe I had this previously untapped, deeply instinctive understanding of cats. Maybe I intuitively "got" cats in a way that other people didn't.

Maybe I was secretly a cat *genius*.

And so, when one of Jorge's sisters announced one Sunday that her mechanic had found a litter of four-week-old kittens, and did any of us know somebody who might want them, I didn't hesitate before claiming one for myself.

It was another two days before Jorge's sister could drive out to her mechanic's garage to pick up the kitten, and I was in a fever pitch of excitement the entire time. For two nights, I tossed in bed with the restlessness of a ten-year-old on Christmas Eve. *A KITTEN is coming! I'm getting a KITTEN!*

I went to the pet store for a litter box and kitten food, and came home with a toy-filled shopping bag so large that I struggled to carry everything up the stairs to our apartment. I'd been an easy mark for the enthusiastic store owner, who'd probably closed up shop and gone home for the day after I left. (I imagined her calling her husband and saying, *Good news, Herb! We can go back to imported wine!*) I'd bought miniature mice by the dozen: some made from felt, some from plastic or sisal rope, some that rattled or squeaked when shaken, some with hidden compartments you could stuff with catnip. I'd gotten a toy that consisted of a circular sisal-rope base with a large metal spring jutting up from it vertically, at the end of which was attached a belled cluster of feathers. There was another circular toy, this one a plastic wheel with a ball trapped inside and slats through which a cat could shove a paw to push the ball around and around in an endless loop. And I'd bought balls in every color of the rainbow: some made of cloth and plush with stuffing, some that whirred and sparkled when pushed, others made from candy-colored plastic. Last but not least, I'd bought a toy worm made from three puffs of cottony material with a little bell attached to one end.

I spent the hour before the kitten arrived arranging this bounty strategically around the apartment as Jorge looked on, until our home resembled a kitty day-care center through which a dozen or so cats might troop at any moment, demanding entertainment.

"They always end up being more interested in the bag the toys came in than the toys themselves, you know," Jorge told me.

I knew that Jorge had far more experience with kittens than I did (I having no experience at all). Still, I silently pooh-poohed him. I knew the kitten would be delighted with this avalanche of playthings—would love the toys not only for their own sakes, but also because of all the love for her and excitement at her arrival that they represented. And we would be so much more than cat and owner, this kitten and I. From the very first look—from the very first *moment*—she and I would form an instant, unbreakable bond and be the best and closest of friends forever. These toys were merely the first step in that process.

At the very least, they certainly brightened up the place. Jorge and I didn't have much in the way of décor in those early days of living together—just a futon, battered coffee table, and highly weathered entertainment center in the living room; a hand-me-down circular plastic table and three chairs in the kitchen area; and another futon along with an ancient dresser in the bedroom. I didn't want the kitten to look around and wonder if maybe her luckier littermates had gone to better, fancier homes, while she'd drawn the losing ticket in the lottery of life.

Cats, I'd been given to understand, could be very judgmental creatures.

I'd barely finished arranging everything just so when the doorbell rang and Jorge's sister entered. She toted a kitten-sized lavender plastic carrier, across the top of which a piece of masking tape with SCARLETT written in black marker had been affixed.

One of the things I'd been looking forward to most was getting to name the kitten. I'd never been the one to name a pet before—with our dogs, that privilege had always fallen to my parents—and I'd seen naming rights as one of the adult prerogatives I would now assume with a cat of my very own.

"She was so dehydrated when the mechanic found her that she kept fainting," Jorge's sister explained. "So he named her Scarlett."

Any disappointment I may have felt upon learning that someone else had already named my kitten dissolved, along with my heart, upon hearing this. *The poor little thing!* I knew I could easily rename her. Young as she was, she wouldn't know the difference. But this name was so closely tied to her origins in life—and the hardships she'd endured before being rescued—that it seemed as if changing it would also erase something important and essential about her.

Scarlett, then, she would be.

Jorge's sister had placed the carrier on the floor at my feet, and I knelt before it, fumbling with the clasp until it sprang open. A tiny black nose poked its way out, quickly followed by the head and body of what was probably the smallest living creature I'd ever been close to.

She was a gray-and-black tiger-striped tabby, with a white belly and chest, white chin, and white "socks" on her lower legs and feet. I marveled at her miniature perfection— the little pink pads of her paws; the tiny, nearly imperceptible tufts of fur sprouting from the tips of her ears; the wee, feathery whiskers on each side of her nose, as if an adult cat's features had been rendered into something small enough to fit in a dollhouse. The next time I went to Jorge's parents' house, only a few days later, their cats would seem to me almost monstrous in size.

Fully emerged from the carrier, the kitten looked at me with wide blue eyes (which would turn a yellowish green in only a few weeks' time). "Hey, Scarlett," I said. I knew I must look like a giantess to her, so I made my voice soft. "Come to your new mama."

This was the moment I'd been waiting for. My mind soared off on flights of quasi- poetic fancy that even now, some twenty years later, I'm embarrassed to remember. This would be a moment of epiphany—a moment when the workings of Destiny (with a capital *D*) would be revealed. That I was about to publicly assume my previously secret identity as "Gwen Cooper, Cat Genius" was a given. Jorge and his sister—and even I, myself—would see that my immediate rapport with Pandy hadn't been a fluke. But it would be more than that, this happening of an instant that was fated to change all our lives. Our eyes would meet, Scarlett's and mine, and that meeting would strike a gong that would resound down through all our remaining years together.

For the merest fraction of a second, Scarlett's blue eyes rested squarely on my own. "Come here, baby," I said encouragingly.

I held my breath, waiting for Scarlett to leap rapturously into my outstretched arms, until my arms began to tire from being extended for so long. But still they remained empty of kitten flesh, rapturous or otherwise.

Scarlett's eyes seemed to glaze over—was I imagining it?—into a look of indifference. She looked at me, and then she looked through me, and then she kitten-waddled *around* me as if I were no more than an inconveniently placed traffic cone.

"Awwwww . . . look at her go!" exclaimed Jorge's sister.

When Scarlett had gotten about five feet away, she flipped suddenly in a kind of half- turn so that she was facing me again. She lifted one of her front paws slightly off the ground as her back arched and her tiny comma of a tail puffed up, and she did a funny little sideways crab walk.

She wants me to play with her, I thought, feeling the beginnings of a smile. Rising to my feet, I hurried over to where she was now standing and hunkered down again, stretching out one hand toward her. "Hi, baby girl!"

For a second time, the kitten turned a blank, wide-eyed gaze in my direction. Then she spun around and scurried off into the bedroom.

Jorge and his sister were watching, and I was painfully aware that the kitten had now rejected me not just once, but twice. But that was silly, I told myself. Of course she hadn't *rejected* me. She was in an entirely new and foreign place, after all—naturally she was a little thrown off. You didn't have to be any kind of a cat expert, secret *or* public, to know that much. So, trying to shift the tenor of my thoughts to more practical matters, I asked Jorge's sister, "Will I need to train her to use the litter box?"

"She'll probably figure it out if you just show her where it is," Jorge's sister replied. She leaned down to pick up her purse, then walked over to give Jorge and me each a peck on the cheek. "I should be getting home," she said. "I still have a half-hour drive ahead of me. Good luck with your new kitten!" she added, aiming a warm smile in my direction, as Jorge walked her downstairs to the parking lot.

We didn't have any big plans for that evening, having set aside the whole night to help our new kitten acclimate. Scarlett reappeared from the bedroom a few minutes later, and I watched as she ran around for a while, keeping an eagle-eyed lookout for any signs of distress or potential hazards that might have gone overlooked when I'd kitten-proofed the apartment. But Scarlett seemed fine in her new home—more than fine. She skittered around for a while, chasing shadows across the floor and invisible bugs up the walls, pausing every so often to impatiently knock one of the cat toys I'd bought out of her way. I crouched down a few more times—trying to get her attention by tapping my fingernails on the tiled floor or tossing a tiny toy ball in her direction—but Scarlett seemed to find my presence as extraneous as she found the toys themselves. Finally, right in the middle of hopping repeatedly into and then out of the shopping bag the toys had come in (thus fulfilling Jorge's prediction), she fell into a deep sleep while still sitting up.

I was pretty tired myself, not having slept much the two nights before. Whenever my family had brought a new puppy into our home, it was always an unspoken rule that the puppy would spend her first night in bed with one of us—born out of a feeling that nobody should spend her first night in a strange place all alone.

And so, as Jorge and I headed into the bedroom, I knelt and gently lifted the sleeping kitten in one hand, marveling at how easily she fit into my palm. It was the first time I'd touched Scarlett. My heart dissolved again at feeling her soft fluff, at seeing up close the little whiskers that swayed gently with her breath, the rise and fall of her tiny, perfect chest.

I carried her into the bedroom and deposited her gently on the bed, lying down next to her once Jorge and I had changed into our pajamas and turned out the lights. I'd thought her likely to sleep all the way through the night, so exhausted did she seem. But, at feeling us settle down next to her, Scarlett awakened, stood up, and bent into a deep, languorous stretch. Then, without so much as a backward glance, she clambered down from the bed and toddled back into the living room. When I checked a few minutes later, I found her asleep in a ball on the couch, her tail wrapped snugly around her nose and forehead.

I couldn't help feeling that the two of us hadn't exactly gotten off to a roaring start.

Still, we were in the early stages of our relationship. It had been unrealistic to expect everything to happen all at once. There would be plenty of time for Scarlett and me to bond, I assured myself, and for that bond to blossom into everything I'd imagined it could be.

After all, tomorrow was another day.

ONE OF THE GREAT charms of living with a dog is that a dog has a way of making you feel as if—unbeknownst to anyone else—you might actually be the greatest person in the world. And not just the greatest, but also the most fascinating. A dog might not understand anything you say beyond her name—from a dog's perspective, your monologues may sound like nothing more than, *Blah blah blah blah*, Casey, *blah blah blah*—but she'll still hang enraptured on your every word like ancient scholars trying to unravel the mysteries of the gods. Even Pandy the cat, in singling me out so decisively, had made me feel as if I just might be special and interesting in ways that I, myself, had never suspected.

Scarlett, however, had none of that particular brand of charm. Scarlett's great power was her ability to make me feel as I might actually be the *least* interesting person that the entirety of human civilization had ever produced.

I would never have said that Scarlett was charm*less*. She was a kitten—she was charming by definition. Everything she did, every gesture she made, every time she chased some microscopic ball of fluff, or raised one miniature paw to her face in a grooming ritual (she was immaculately clean, my Scarlett was), or rubbed a fuzzy cheek against a table leg or door frame to mark it with her scent, I was charmed. I was enthralled. Seeing her play and gambol about was an endless source of fascination.

I may have been fascinated by all things Scarlett, but Scarlett couldn't have been less fascinated by me. Watching her scamper around—as happy and healthy as any kitten, despite the ordeal of her earliest life—I wanted nothing more than to cuddle and play with her, to entertain her and find new ways of increasing her joy.

But if I walked into a room, Scarlett would either walk out of it or continue whatever she'd been doing with barely a glance in my direction. If she was asleep on the bed at night when I got into it, she'd wake up just long enough to hop down and head off to sleep on the living room couch. Or, if she was asleep on the couch and I sat down next to her—even if I sat all the way at the other end, as far from her as possible so as to avoid disturbing her catnap—she'd promptly decamp for the bedroom and snooze in there.

"Seriously—what the hell?" I said to Jorge one day, as we watched Scarlett unceremoniously exit a room we'd just entered and I fought the sudden impulse to sniff under my arms for offensive body odor.

Her kitten fluff, which refused to lie flat no matter how strenuously she tried to lick it into place, was a sore temptation for my fingers. How I longed to feel the warmth and softness of her fuzzy little body! Scarlett didn't shrink from my touch, exactly, when I tried to pet her, nor did she violently lash out. Rather, she took no visible notice of my caresses one way or the other. She'd just kind of slide out from under my hand, like someone absent-mindedly brushing lint from their shoulder, and trot off to do something else.

That she took no interest in the treasure trove of toys I'd bought her probably goes without saying. I'd dangle a little felt mouse enticingly by its tail over her head, and she wouldn't even muster a half-hearted swipe at it. I'd bend the vertical spring attached to the sisal-rope base until its feathered-and-belled crest touched the floor, then let it spring back to make the feathers flutter and the bell tinkle merrily. "Look, Scarlett!" I'd say in my best talking-to-a-kitten voice. (It was very similar to my sing-songy talking-to-a-dog voice.) Widening my eyes to feign great astonishment, I'd say, "What's *this*, Scarlett? What's *this*?"

That voice had never failed to rouse even the sleepiest dog to near frenzies of tail-wagging, hand-licking, and playful crouching. Even Pandy always responded to it with louder purrs and spirited Siamese mews of acknowledgment.

Scarlett, however, would merely level a bored gaze in my direction. *It's a bunch of feathers, stupid.* And that was all the response I'd get.

"At least *somebody's* playing with them," Jorge observed, coming home one day to find me flat on my belly in front of Scarlett, a cat toy in each hand, absorbed in yet another fruitless attempt to engage her attentions.

"Don't you dare say *I told you so*," I warned him.

Naturally Scarlett liked to play—she was a kitten, after all. When she wasn't sleeping or eating, playing was all she did. She chased her tiny tail in dizzying circles until she appeared little more than a gray-and-white blur. She would frequently do that sideways flip and crab-walk that I'd come to call "Ninja kitty." She found bits of dust or tufts of her own shed fur and chased them furiously from one end of the apartment to the other, or sat up on her hind legs like a prairie dog and tried to catch the dust motes that appeared like flecks of gold in the sunbeams that fell through the windows.

Scarlett's favorite game of all was to chase a crumpled-up ball of paper around the room, batting it furiously between her front paws and then knocking it just far enough out of reach that she'd have to run after it. It was her favorite game, that is, if she happened to find the wadded paper ball on her own. If, however, I obligingly crumpled up a new piece and tossed it over to her, she'd watch the paper ball as it rolled to a stop at her feet and then stare at me, as if wondering why an apparently sane person would throw garbage around her own home.

Scarlett had, at a minimum, caught on to the fact that it was I, and not Jorge, who was her primary caregiver. As the weeks passed and her kittenish cheeps matured into more adult-sounding tones, she developed what Jorge and I called "Scarlett's mother-in-law voice," a harsh, guttural, and distinctly unloving meow that sounded like *MRAAAAAAA* and was deployed only when Scarlett felt she had something to complain about. And I was the only one she ever complained to.

When her food bowl was empty, for example, or her litter box was dirty—even as a kitten, Scarlett had exacting standards when it came to litter box maintenance—I was the one who heard about it. "*MRAAAAAAA*," Scarlett would say, sitting on her haunches on the floor directly in front of me if I was on the couch watching TV. If I didn't jump up immediately to attend to her, she'd advance to the coffee table, making sure to position herself directly between me and my view of the TV screen. "*MRAAAAAAA*," she'd repeat. "*MRAAAAAAA!*" If I was reading a book with my legs stretched out, she'd sit on my knees until the pressure of her weight made the joints ache and demand, "*MRAAAAAAA.*" And if I didn't look up from my book quickly enough, she would put one paw directly onto the page I was reading, insisting at the top of her voice, "*MRAAAAAAA!!!*"

"All *right!*" I'd finally say, getting up and scurrying off to attend to whatever it was that was bothering her. "You know," I suggested once, looking back at her over my shoulder, "it wouldn't kill you to say something *nice* every once in a while."

To Jorge, Scarlett paid literally no attention at all—and he, after a few attempts at petting her or tossing her paper balls, was content to let her go her own way without any further interference. "Some cats just don't like people," he said.

He was right, of course. There were cats who flat-out didn't like humans. Nevertheless, it struck me as a premature judgment in Scarlett's case. She was still so little! She'd been only four weeks old when we'd gotten her—and she was barely twelve weeks old now. Surely, a kitten rescued at such a young age, and adopted immediately into a loving home, should be capable of forming an emotional bond with *someone*.

I felt vindicated a few days later when, sitting on the couch, I felt a tickling at the back of my head. Twisting my neck just a fraction so I could see her from the corner of my eye, I observed Scarlett sitting behind me on the futon's arm, her face buried deep in my hair as she nuzzled gently and insistently. I remembered my mother telling stories like this about Tippi, a little beagle/terrier mix she and my father had adopted before I was born. Tippi had been so attached to my mother as a puppy that she'd insisted on sleeping each night on my mother's pillow, nestled in her hair.

Awwww, I thought, and my heart began to puddle—what could this new behavior of Scarlett's be if not, at long last, an affectionate gesture? *I knew I was right!* I thought, and decided not to say anything to Jorge—not right away, at least. I'd let him discover the two of us like this on his own one day. I tried reaching my hand slowly back and around to stroke Scarlett's fur as she pressed her nose and whiskers all the way into my scalp. But she wriggled out impatiently from under my touch, and—not wanting to push her too far, too quickly—I left her to it, murmuring, *Good Scarlett... sweet kitty...*

This went on for some days, and I began to cast a complacent eye over Scarlett as she tore around the apartment, absorbed in her play. I still longed to rub beneath her little white chin and hear her purr of contentment, to watch her stir and sigh as she fell asleep in my lap or curled up next to my leg. She wasn't yet what anyone might call demonstrative, aside from those moments she spent buried in my hair. But a good time was coming—I could feel it. We were finally starting to bond, my kitten and I, and the rest would happen in its own time.

All that newfound complacency was shattered a couple of weeks later, however, when I happened to catch a glimpse of Scarlett in my peripheral vision, sitting behind me with a thick lock of my hair—*which she'd gnawed off my head*—hanging from her jaws.

"What the—" I sat bolt upright, the book in my hands tumbling to the floor. "Is *that* what you've been doing this whole time?!"

I'd been blessed (or cursed, depending on Miami's up-and-down humidity) with an extraordinarily full head of hair—enough that I hadn't noticed from one day to the next as bits of it had begun to disappear. But now, disbelieving at first, I reached around and felt what I realized was a decidedly thinning patch on the back of my head.

I told myself to stay calm. After all, was it even *possible* for one smallish kitten to chew a bald spot right into a person's scalp?

With mounting horror—as I clutched at a limp clump of wispy strands that had, only recently, been a thick tangle of curls—I decided that, yes . . . yes, it was.

"*Oye!*" I cried. "*No se hace!*" (Jorge and his family disciplined their own cats in Spanish, and I'd fallen into the habit myself.) "*Malo gato!*" I shouted. "*MALO GATO!*"

Startled, Scarlett leapt from the couch and I chased her, trying to wrest the lock of my hair from her mouth. Obviously I didn't think I could stick it back on, but at least I could stop her from swallowing it, if that was indeed her plan. After about three minutes of pursuit—she nimbly evading my grasp, I feeling more than a little ridiculous to be lumbering so ineffectually after a *kitten,* for crying out loud—she darted under the bed and out of my reach.

She emerged a little while later but ignored me for the rest of the day, not even bothering with the litany of complaints she usually took up around twenty minutes before her dinnertime. The small pot of cat grass I bought the next day—as a more suitable source of fiber, as well as a gesture of reconciliation (*like an erring husband coming home with flowers,* I thought wryly)—remained untouched.

STRICT HONESTY COMPELS ME to say that there actually *was* one game Scarlett enjoyed playing with me—although describing it that way requires loose definitions of the words *game, play,* and *with.* The "game," such as it was, consisted of Scarlett hiding behind a table leg, or underneath the couch or bed, and leaping out at me as I walked past. She'd hurl herself at my ankles, latching on with her teeth and front claws while her back claws kicked at me furiously, "bunny feet" style, until she drew blood, or I tripped and fell, or both.

I wore heels to work every day. I didn't have the greatest balance in them, and I was always terrified when Scarlett jumped at me that a pointy heel might inadvertently puncture her head or vulnerable belly. In the process of trying to quickly shuffle my feet away from Scarlett and remain upright at the same time, it wasn't at all unusual for me to end up tumbling to the ground, falling heavily against whatever piece of furniture Scarlett had just jumped out at me from. I bruised rather easily, and my arms, shoulders, and chest were soon spotted with incriminating black-and-blue marks.

It couldn't really be said that Scarlett played this game of hers "with" me, because if I made any attempt to touch or even look at her, the game was immediately over, and off she'd run. And even describing it as "play" seems inapt, because Scarlett's surprise attacks didn't feel playful so much as . . . mean-spirited. How else could I describe it? Whenever I hit the tiled floor of our apartment with a loud "Oof!" I always sensed that Scarlett was enjoying a silent kitten laugh at my expense. *It's funny when humans fall down!*

Still, I was pathetically pleased at receiving even this much attention from my otherwise aloof feline. Like her complaining, this was something else Scarlett did only with me—never with Jorge. Maybe it was true, I reflected (trying not to notice how desperately I was grasping at straws), that you only hurt the ones you love.

Things came to a head one day at work. The school-based community service program I ran was considered a crime prevention initiative, and our administrative space— located in a small office park in southwest Miami—had been donated by the Miami police department. Our next-door neighbor was the bomb squad, and I spent many a happy work break in our shared parking lot, watching as the puppies who were being trained to sniff out explosives bonded with their handlers.

On this particular day, I'd taken off my blazer in the heat of a broiling afternoon, and the sleeveless silk top I wore underneath left my battered arms bared. I didn't really think about it until one of the bomb-squad officers I was friendly with—a six-foot-two wall of muscle named Eddie del Toro—followed me through reception and into my private office as I returned from lunch, closing the door behind him. Startled at this unprecedented behavior, I turned to face him with a question mark clearly written in my raised eyebrows.

Eddie took one of my hands gently in his own, looked earnestly into my eyes, and said in a soft, reassuring voice:

"Just tell me his name and where I can find him."

This has gone far enough, I told myself a few minutes later, as I stalked out to my car to retrieve my discarded blazer. Naturally I'd understood the conclusions Eddie had reached upon seeing my bruises—and why his first thought had been *abusive boyfriend* and not *evil kitten*. I'd explained to him about Scarlett, but I'd still had to show off the corroborating itty-bitty claw marks on my ankles, and then exaggeratedly mime tripping over a small cat a few times, before I'd finally been able to send Officer Eddie—laughing and shaking his head— back over to the bomb squad.

Things were getting ridiculous. I didn't intend to start going around in turtlenecks and wigs to cover up bruises and bald patches inflicted upon me *by a kitten*, as if I were the hapless heroine in a Lifetime movie. Something about an abusive, emotionally unavailable cat and the woman who couldn't help loving her anyway. *Seduced by a Feline,* I thought. *A Kitten to Die For: The Scarlett Cooper Story.*

I headed to Barnes & Noble after work that evening and bought an advice book about kittens. Once I was home, I turned immediately to the chapter on how to deal with early signs of aggression. The book advised that, should your kitten show a tendency to attack you in overly aggressive play, you should say *No!* in a firm voice, and then provide the kitten with an appropriate toy as a substitute for your own flesh.

"No!" I said to Scarlett the next time she leapt out at me from under the coffee table. Reaching down carefully to remove her, claw by claw, from around my ankle, I held out one of the neglected toy mice that had been gathering dust in the corners of our apartment these past three months. "*Here,*" I told her firmly, "is your appropriate toy."

Scarlett looked at the felt mouse in my hand with an air of disdain. Then, with all the

offended dignity of a society matron in a state of high dudgeon, she turned her little rump to me and strode away, swishing her tail twice to emphasize her displeasure. This silent treatment lasted until Scarlett's next surprise attack—which happened about fifteen minutes later.

It was a pattern we repeated four or five times over the course of the night, always with the same results. The book advised that, if all else failed, the best way to break a cat of aggressive habits was simply to ignore her. When she wrapped herself around one of my ankles, I should detach her and then disregard her. I wasn't to talk to her, pet her, try to engage her in play, or even so much as look at her. There was no worse punishment for a playful young kitten, the book assured me, than being denied interactive play time with her human.

"HA!" I exclaimed when I read this. The next day, I dropped the book off at the Salvation Army donation bin.

I TOLD MYSELF THAT Scarlett was just independent—and, moreover, that being independent was a good thing. I was a little fuzzy as to why, exactly, independence was a desirable quality in a companion animal. (It wasn't as if I were preparing Scarlett to pursue an equitable marriage or high-powered career someday.) Still, "independent" was one of those generically positive descriptors—like "attractive" or "has good taste"—that most people were pleased to have applied to themselves. Why wouldn't I want it applied to my cat?

I also told myself—and actually knew, deep down at the bottom of things—that it wasn't Scarlett's job in life to interact with me in any specific manner, or to make me feel a certain way about myself. Our relationship was based on what *my* job was—and it was my job to keep her healthy and safe, to love her no matter what her personality turned out to be, and to give her everything she needed to live a happy life on her own terms.

But what if, I sometimes wondered, I simply wasn't able to give her that happy life? What if Scarlett and I had been mismatched—what if the reason she hadn't yet "chosen" me was because she'd been meant for somebody else, and I'd interfered somehow in her destiny? Maybe Scarlett's true human soulmate—a person who could make her happier than I ever could—was still out there, forever to remain undiscovered.

It would be a gross mischaracterization of our relationship to say that it was all bad, that I didn't love her, or even that I wished I'd gotten another kitten instead. The truth was, I'd fallen irretrievably in love with this bossy, snooty, semi-sadistic little imp who—when she wasn't tormenting me or demanding something from me—seemed otherwise uninterested in my existence.

I didn't love her just because she was mine (although that—as with any other parent, cat or otherwise—would have been enough to raise Scarlett above all other kittens in my eyes). I loved the little freckle of black fur, which I called "Scarlett's beauty mark," resting on the left side of her upper lip. I loved the way she cocked her head thoughtfully to one side before leaping at a paper ball. I loved the serious, evaluating expression she wore as she sniffed at some new variety of food I put before her when she outgrew her kitten food. I loved the little sway of her backside as she walked away from me in a huff.

When she developed a large sore on her lower lip—the result of a feline herpes virus she'd inherited at birth from her mother, which would plague her on and off for the rest of her life—I fussed and fretted and dragged her to the vet (which didn't exactly raise me in Scarlett's esteem), and mixed the icky pink antibiotic formula the doctor prescribed with some water from a can of tuna, trying to make it more palatable. I'd give her some of the tuna itself afterward to get the yucky-medicine taste out of her mouth, as miserable over her obvious discomfort as if it were my own.

Sometimes, watching Scarlett nap peacefully on a pillow in a patch of sunlight, surrounded by toys she didn't seem to care about—representing a love she didn't seem interested in—I thought about what might have become of her if she hadn't been rescued or found a home. I often took my teenage volunteers to local animal shelters, and had spoken with their staffers enough to know the kinds of things that happened to very small kittens left to fend for themselves on the streets. That Scarlett had been saved against all the odds— that she now had the privilege of being indifferent, if she chose, to a human who provided her with food and shelter and love—seemed like a kind of miracle. My cat was daily proof, in my own home, of goodness in the world. How could I not have loved her?

There are two sides to every story, and I'm sure that Scarlett would have had her own list of complaints about me if she'd been able to talk. She tries too hard, Scarlett might have said. She intrudes on the games I like to play by myself. I can't even stretch out comfortably on my back without her trying to rub the white fur of my belly—as if I were a *dog*! She disappears for hours from the apartment every day, and then turns up again whenever she feels like it. And she expects me to *cheer* about it like it's a big deal! She hogs the pillows on the bed. She'll open a can of tuna and, sure, she'll give me a *little*—but she still keeps most of it for herself.

One night Jorge and I were watching a re-run of *The Simpsons* on TV. It was a Valentine's Day episode, and Lisa Simpson had, as an act of pity, given a Valentine's card to a slow-witted boy named Ralph, whom nobody else in the second-grade class had even acknowledged. "I choo-choo-*choose* you!" Ralph read ecstatically from Lisa's card, which was decorated with a drawing of a smiley-faced train engine.

Crazy as it sounds, I was envious of that slow-witted little boy. He'd been chosen, and I had not.

It had been May when we first adopted Scarlett, and it was November when my boss sent me to attend a three-day national conference for youth outreach programs like ours.

Although the conference was being held in Miami, the downtown hotel where I'd be staying was far enough away to make it impractical for me to get home to feed Scarlett twice a day. Jorge traveled frequently for work and was scheduled to be away himself that entire week. We couldn't find a pet-sitter willing to come all the way out to our neighborhood for what we could afford to pay, so Jorge's parents offered to take Scarlett for a couple of nights.

I arrived at their house early on the morning of the first day of the conference to get Scarlett and her gear—her litter box and extra litter, cans of food, her water and food bowls, her scratching post, her brush, her antibiotic medication in case her herpes flared up in my absence, and a few toys—set up in the guest bedroom. With its adjoining bathroom, Scarlett would have free run of a space nearly as large as our apartment. Keeping her separated from the other three cats—and especially from Targa—meant she would spend most of her time shut in by herself, except when Maggie could slip in for feedings and visits. Given how much Scarlett seemed to crave solitude, however, I didn't think she'd mind a few days of extra alone time. She'd probably see it as a vacation.

Scarlett sprang from her carrier as soon as I opened it. I'd spent half an hour that morning chasing her around the apartment to get her *into* it, and the fresh claw mark on my hand attested to just how reluctant to travel Scarlett had been. I tried to give her a conciliatory scratch behind the ears with that same hand now, but the decidedly cool manner in which Scarlett shook me off let me know that I hadn't been forgiven. Exploring the room with her little black nose to the ground, she seemed reassured to find so many things with her own familiar scent on them.

The window in Scarlett's room overlooked the driveway, and as I headed out to my car I saw her sitting on the sill, watching me. I crept over and, with one finger, lightly rubbed the glass over the bridge of Scarlett's nose. "It's only a few days," I told her. "I'll be back for you soon."

Scarlett opened her mouth wide in a mighty yawn, then hopped down from the windowsill and disappeared from sight.

I thought about her in between conference sessions during those three days and called Maggie both nights to see how Scarlett was doing. I'd be lying, though, if I said I worried about her much. Scarlett's independence—her apparent indifference to me, specifically, and humanity in general—had become an accepted fact. There would be someone to feed her while I was gone, and to clean up after her, and she'd have her little paper balls and the stuffed worm—the only store-bought toy in which Scarlett had shown even the remotest interest—to play with. What more had she ever really needed?

This assessment seemed borne out by Maggie's reports when I called to check in. "I haven't heard a peep out of her," Maggie told me. "If I didn't already know she was here, I'd never guess there was another cat in the house." She added that Scarlett would retreat under the bed whenever Maggie entered the room, or else head for the bathroom where she could watch from an untouchable distance as Maggie put down food and cleaned out used litter.

"Don't take it personally," I told her. "Scarlett doesn't like people all that much." I realized, as I said it, that I'd been secretly angry at Jorge for saying something not very different, not so very long ago.

I'd dropped Scarlett off at Jorge's parents' house on a Wednesday morning, and it was around five o'clock on Friday afternoon when I arrived to pick her up. Jorge's parents had their own architectural firm and often worked long hours, and the house was empty as I let myself in with the key Maggie had lent me. Jorge's sister had been by earlier to release Targa into the backyard, and I poked my head out to say hi to her—and, of course, I stopped to give Pandy an affectionate hello as well.

"Hey, *Scarlettsita bonita*!" (Spanish for "pretty little Scarlett") I called cheerfully as I opened the door to the guest room. Scarlett leapt from the bed and ran over to where I stood, stopping a few inches away to sit on her haunches and look up into my face with bright-eyed anticipation. Scarlett had never once greeted me at the door like this— preferring, as always, to evacuate any room as I entered—although at the time I didn't register how unusual her behavior was. My mind was too occupied trying to figure out the most efficient way to get Scarlett and all her things loaded into the car, and a route home that would avoid the worst of Friday rush-hour traffic. There was too much for me to carry out in one trip, so I decided to load Scarlett's gear into the car's trunk and backseat first, and then I'd return to the house to put Scarlett herself in her carrier and bring her out.

I had just slammed the lid of the trunk shut over the litter box when I heard it. The wild howling of an animal in great distress rose—sudden and sharp—to cut like a band saw through the peaceful tweeting of birds and humming of insects in the glowing, late-afternoon air.

Jorge's parents lived at the end of a quiet cul-de-sac, just beyond which lay a wooded copse. There were a few feral cats who lived among the trees who Maggie had arranged to have spayed and neutered some time back, and who she still continued to feed. They reminded me of Scarlett, with their tiger stripes and yellow-green eyes, and their persistent wariness of any human contact. Every so often they would emerge to sunbathe on the hot asphalt of the driveway, and I was always careful when I drove up to the house to make sure the coast was clear before pulling in.

My first, awful thought now was that, despite my precautions, I might have run one of them over. My stomach rose into my throat as I knelt on hands and knees to look beneath my car. Thankfully, there was nothing there.

Loud as they were, the howls had a curiously muffled sound. Maybe a stowaway had crept unnoticed into the trunk or backseat as I'd packed in Scarlett's things? But a thorough check of both revealed nothing. I also examined the wheel wells of all four tires and popped the hood to see if a cat, or some other small animal, might have crawled in to doze on the warmth of the engine and gotten trapped.

Nothing.

The howls sounded close by, but I couldn't find anything in or around my car to account for them. As I slammed the hood and doors shut, however, they escalated in both urgency and pitch. Thoroughly mystified, I stood in the middle of the driveway and turned in a slow circle, nerving myself to venture into the darkening woods for further investigation if I didn't spot anything immediately obvious.

The glare of the setting sun off the guest bedroom window, which had previously obscured my view inside, receded a little. And that's when I saw her.

Scarlett was on the windowsill. She stood high on her back legs, her front paws clawing desperately at the glass. She was looking directly at me; when our eyes met, she threw back her head and opened her mouth wide, yowling at the top of her lungs.

"*Scarlett!*" I cried. "Scarlett, I'm coming!"

For the second time, I felt my throat tighten and my stomach clench. I had no idea what was wrong with Scarlett—my only thought was that some unknown, terrible thing was happening to her. My hands shook, and I nearly dropped my keys as I fumbled with the lock to the front door of the house. I raced down the hall toward the guest room, nearly tripping over the purse I'd set down upon entering, and flung the bedroom door open.

Scarlett broke off mid-yowl when I came in, and the abrupt silence was as piercing as her cries had been. She leapt from the windowsill to land at my feet, whirling and dipping in frantic figure eights in front of me. At the head of each loop, she paused to rub furiously against my ankles from her cheek to her hip before resuming her spins once again.

I saw no blood, no swelling, no limping or hobbling, nothing to indicate any kind of injury or illness. I hadn't seen any sign of the other three cats when I came into the house, and I guessed they'd gone into deep hiding when the howling started. At any rate, they hadn't gotten into Scarlett's room to attack or upset her. Targa remained securely in the yard; I'd caught a glimpse of her sitting at attention just outside the glass door that led out back, looking anxiously into the house as a low whine rose in her throat. Clearly, Scarlett's cries had disturbed her, too.

"Hey," I said, gently. "Hey, Scarlett." I crouched down and reached out to her. I wanted to pet her, to try to calm her with the touch of my hand. But I hesitated. When had the touch of my hand ever meant anything to Scarlett?

To my surprise, Scarlett half-rose on her hind legs so that her head met my hand in midair. I tentatively scratched along the side of her neck and lower jaw, and she turned to press her whole face into my palm.

I lowered my body further until I sat cross-legged on the floor, facing Scarlett with my back against the bedroom door I'd closed behind me. She sat down on her haunches facing me, and as I continued to scratch gently along her neck and jaw, her eyelids drooped, and the low, rumbling sound of her purr rose to fill the room.

It was the first time Scarlett had ever purred when I touched her.

"Did you think I was leaving without you?" I asked softly. And I realized, as I said it, that that was exactly what Scarlett had thought. She'd seen me walk out with all her things, and then she'd heard the slam of the car door, and she'd assumed that the next sound she would hear was the car engine as I drove away and left her behind.

My fingers paused in their scratching, and I cupped Scarlett's face in my hand. She regarded me solemnly with her luminous, inscrutable yellow-green eyes.

I leaned forward slightly, to make my own eyes level with hers. "I will *never* leave you," I told her. "Not ever. You and I are stuck with each other. Okay?"

I didn't expect a reply, of course, and I didn't get one. Instead, Scarlett stretched out her front legs and her neck, until her belly rested on the floor and her chin rested on my ankle. Then she closed her eyes. The vibrations of her purr soon gave way to the steadier rhythms of her breath as she fell asleep.

The room grew dim in the gathering dusk, and I reached up to flip the wall light switch that would turn on the bedside lamp. The fur of Scarlett's neck was soft on my ankle, and I lowered my arm to stroke her back.

I waited for my legs to stiffen, to feel my arm growing tired or the weight of Scarlett's head becoming uncomfortable on my ankle. But that never happened. The warmth and drowsiness of Scarlett's sleeping body seemed to seep into my own, and all I felt was a sense of balm. Balm and ease. The feeling that a tiny, twinging knot, which I'd lived with long enough to have stopped noticing it, had finally begun to loosen.

"Good Scarlett," I murmured. "Good, good girl."

We sat together like that, in the amber circle of lamplight, for a long time.

THINGS CHANGED BETWEEN US after that, although not dramatically, and not right away. Scarlett most certainly did not become a lap cat. She didn't start running over whenever I called her. There was never a moment when Jorge looked at the two of us together and said, *Look how affectionate Scarlett's become! You're a miracle worker!*

In May of the following year, when Scarlett was a year old, we adopted another kitten—a tiny white fluff-ball only five weeks old, who'd been found wandering the streets of Little Haiti alone, near where my mother taught elementary school. My mother called me in tears over this half-starved, mite-ridden creature, who she couldn't bring home with her but couldn't bear to leave. So the kitten came to live with us, and I named her Vashti. Vashti was an affectionate cuddle-bug right from the start—and while Scarlett was initially a reluctant big sister, it wasn't long before Vashti's gentle sweetness won her over. Having a kitten to boss around put an end, once and for all, to Scarlett's game of "let's trip Mom and make her fall down!"

I don't know when exactly it happened, although I do know that it was well before a month-old, permanently blind kitten named Homer, adopted more than a year after Vashti, came to complete our little family. Maybe it was seeing Vashti so frequently snuggled into my lap or curled up with me in bed that gave Scarlett the idea. But I began to notice how sometimes, waking up in the morning, I'd find Scarlett on our bed, fast asleep between my ankles. Or I'd be reading a book on the couch and Scarlett would come to stretch out across the top of the sofa behind my head—mercifully leaving my hair alone, but resting one small white paw on my shoulder and purring as she nodded off. Before Homer came to rewrite all the old rules, it was Scarlett who was the first to greet me at the door every day when I came home from work—even if she didn't do much more than quickly brush her head against my ankles and then run off before I could pet her.

And it was Scarlett, when Jorge and I finally broke up for good after nearly four years together, who followed me as I got into bed that first, agonizing night, curling up on the empty pillow next to mine as I cried myself to sleep. When I awakened in the morning, feeling somehow warm and calm even as I remembered what had happened the day before, I realized that Scarlett was lying across my chest. Her heart beat against my own, and her head nuzzled into the crook of my neck as she purred gently into my ear. It was as if she'd known that the hardest thing about that first morning would be waking up by myself, and she was telling me that even without Jorge, I wasn' t alone.

Insofar as Scarlett became affectionate at all, it was only ever with me. Her disdain for humanity as a general concept would remain with her for the rest of her life. Scarlett was always the cat who immediately left the room when people came over, who would reject— with claws and teeth, if necessary—anybody else's attempts to pet her. She would always be the cat who required an explanation. *You shouldn't touch Scarlett. You definitely shouldn't try to pet Scarlett. Maybe it's best if you don't even look at Scarlett.* After Jorge and I had ended things, when I lived for a few years on South Beach—and unexpectedly found myself part of a tightly knit, somewhat snobbish nightlife scene, whose glittering VIP rooms were closely guarded against any incursion by the "hoi polloi"—I would warn visiting friends, with a certain mock hauteur, "Scarlett is *very* exclusive." And they would eye her with respect, grasping something fundamental—and, in its way, endearing—about Scarlett's nature in far less time than it had taken me. It was, after all, undeniably flattering to be the one and only human permitted into a highly selective cat's inner life.

All that's jumping ahead, though. What did change immediately—right then on that November day when I picked up Scarlett at Jorge's parents' house—was my realization that Scarlett knew who I was, beyond just a hand that dispensed food or scooped out a litter box. She knew who I was *to her*. It mattered—more than either of us had known—that the hand feeding or cleaning up after her was *my* hand and nobody else's.

Maybe Scarlett and I hadn't "chosen" each other, exactly. There never was that one magical moment, the meeting of eyes, the resounding gong of two souls' instant recognition of each other. What Scarlett and I had was, as it turned out, something far more elusive and enduring than that. It wasn't the sort of thing that sprang up in a flash; it had to develop quietly, through months and years of love, patience, and growing trust.

The world may have been filled with other cats who would have come when I called or cuddled in my lap or slept every night next to me in bed. And it may also have been filled with other humans who could empty a can of food into Scarlett's dish and then leave her alone, just as easily as I could.

At the rock-solid core of things, however, there was only one me for Scarlett, and there was only one Scarlett for me.

And that was enough. It was more than enough. It was everything.

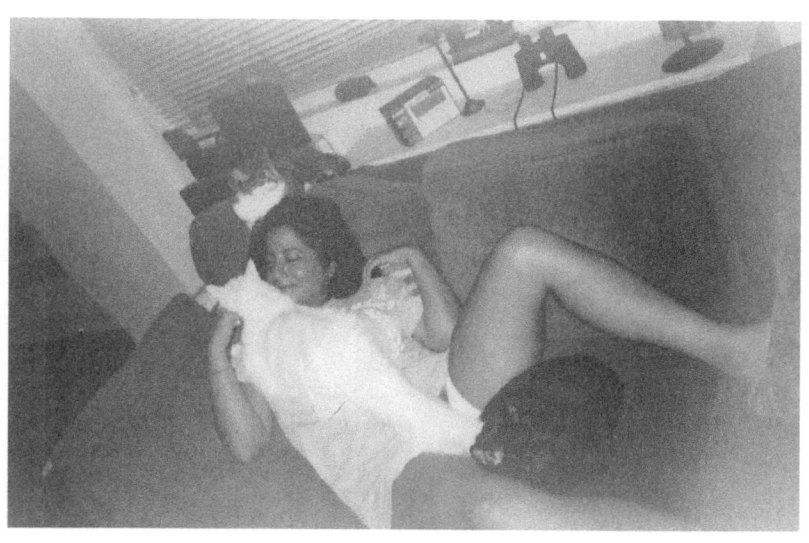

Getting There is Half the Fun

I WAS READING A book recently (*The Friend*, by Sigrid Nunez) in which a doctor acquaintance of the narrator explains to her that during the psychiatric rotation of his residency, he'd been taught that having multiple cats could be a sign of mental illness. Observing that one does occasionally hear about cat hoarders, and expressing a general approval that this was something health-care professionals were being trained to look out for, the narrator asked her doctor friend what number of cats would be considered the "tipping point" as a possible indicator of insanity. And the doctor replied, "Three."

I was glad that I first encountered this in the privacy of my home and not, say, sitting in a bookstore audience somewhere, hearing the author read it aloud. I'm positive that I would have laughed long and hard (as I did when reading it to myself), and maybe it would have been one of those uncomfortable moments where you're the only one laughing in a roomful of silent, serious people. Because maybe "three" wasn't supposed to be the punch line of a joke. Maybe it wasn't a joke at all. Or maybe it was, but the joke was on *us*—the "crazy cat people" of the world (*Look at those wacky people with as many as three cats!*).

I mean, c'mon ... *three?!* Three is nothing! In my world—being in daily contact with any number of people who work in animal rescue—it almost isn't even worth noting how many cats a person has until the number gets into double digits. And even then, so long as that number doesn't climb much above a baker's dozen, and you live in a home sufficiently large to give everyone their space, you're probably okay. Two of my closest friends live on a hobby farm in Tennessee with *eleven* cats—along with eight cows, four horses, a constantly fluctuating number of chickens, an apiary full of honeybees, and one three-legged dog. As a long-time urban apartment dweller, I've always loved hearing their "crazy" stories about life on the farm. But I've never thought of them as being *actually* crazy.

Still, I'd be lying if I said that there were never days, back when I had my "first generation" of three cats—Scarlett, Vashti, and Homer—when I felt like I might be cracking up, or wondered if maybe I needed to have my own head examined. It was possible that I'd gone 'round the bend a long time ago, and that my friends secretly wished I'd get myself to a therapist's office posthaste without their having to intervene.

This impulse to consult a trained psychiatric professional was never stronger than on days, like the one back in 2005, when I had to take all three cats to the vet's office at the same time.

A three-cat vet visit was a physically unwieldy and decidedly unpleasant eventuality that I tried to avoid whenever possible. Although I'd adopted my cats over a three-year period, each a year apart from the other, their birthdays fell close together on the calendar—May for Scarlett and Vashti, and July for Homer (peak "kitten season" months, as anyone in rescue will tell you). This meant that the timing of their annual physicals also fell close together. Nevertheless, it was worth the effort of making two or three separate trips rather than bringing them in simultaneously.

Just getting the three of them into their carriers all at once was an ordeal. I had to take the carriers out of the closet the night before I planned to use them, because Scarlett and Vashti would go into deep hiding for hours once the carriers made an appearance. (I think Homer knew they were there, but maybe they didn't freak him out because he was blind and thus couldn't see them.) Right before I planned to load them in, I had to lure the cats into the living room/kitchen area with a rattling cat-treat bag and then close the doors of bedrooms and bathrooms, once they'd assembled and gotten their first round of treats, to bar any potential escape routes. Homer would happily munch away on his, blissfully unaware of what was about to happen. But as each door in the apartment closed one by one, with the three carriers looming in a row before them, the expressions on the faces of the other two cats would flicker from surprised gratitude (*hey! treats!*) to betrayed wariness (*oh . . . that's why we're getting treats*).

I always started with Vashti, because she was, surprisingly, the most difficult to catch. I'd spend a good five minutes chasing her up and down the hallway; over, around, and behind the furniture; and underneath the dining-room table—requiring me to shove it out of the way and thus allowing her to escape (a ruse I invariably fell for). I always heard the *Benny Hill* "Yakety Sax" music playing in my head as my fleet-footed feline nimbly evaded my grasp time after time, her fluffy white tail flying out behind her like a comet, until—with a desperate lunge—I'd snatch her up at last. Once caught, while I tried to hold the soft carrier open with one hand and shove her into it with the other, Vashti would splay out her hind legs like a jackrabbit, thwarting my efforts by making herself too wide to fit through the carrier's opening. By the time I finally managed to prop the bag open with enough stability that it stayed that way on its own, one of my hands holding Vashti's rear legs together and the other firmly clutching the scruff of her neck as I wrangled her into it, I was already panting and exhausted—and I still had two cats to go.

Scarlett was on the chubby side and, although she'd put up a token effort at running away, far easier to catch. Still, her wild hisses and snarls as I corralled her into her carrier informed me in no uncertain terms that I was the Cruella De Vil of cat moms. Homer, who never shied away from confrontation, didn't run away at all. Once I had him in my hands, he simply transformed himself—Tasmanian Devil-like—into a whirling mass of fur and claws. I didn't so much place Homer in his carrier as blindly aim him in its general direction, holding him out at full arm's length, until the physics of it aligned by pure chance and he was somehow safely inside, slashing frantically and popping his head out through the opening to the last as I held him down and zipped the flap shut above him.

(A few years later, I would make the mistake of scheduling a routine vet appointment for Homer ten days before my wedding—and then spend those ten days with my hands covered in honey, because I'd read someplace that honey helped wounds heal faster, and the uncomfortable stickiness of it, even amid all the last-minute stress of wedding planning, still seemed preferable to standing up in front of everyone I knew, in my exquisitely pristine gown, while Laurence tenderly placed a wedding ring onto a hand as scraped and scabby as a tomboy's kneecaps.)

Even under normal circumstances, I was never at my coiffed and perfumed best by the time I finally sank into a chair in the vet's waiting room. But this particular day had been far from normal. My hair was frizzed up to outrageous heights, my mascara had puddled in black pools under my eyes, and I don't know if you could really call what was happening on my sweat-soaked shirt "pit stains," given that the wet patches radiated out from my actual armpits to meet in the middle of my chest.

And their exams hadn't even started yet! Vashti was a good-enough patient (she'd struggle a bit, but ultimately let the doctors and techs do whatever they needed to do without a fight). Scarlett and Homer, however, were not. Homer was a thoroughly bad patient, truth be told. The only shot I had at keeping him calm enough for the exam even to take place without some hapless vet tech's getting hurt was to hold his carrier in my lap while we sat in the waiting room. Accordingly, I now had one wounded hand inserted through the flap of its zip-up top to gently stroke his head. I'd arranged Scarlett and Vashti on the chairs on each side of me, turned so they could see me smile at them reassuringly through the front mesh of their carriers.

But they all knew where they were—even Homer, who may have been blind, but still knew exactly what a vet's office smelled like. The three of them wailed their misery to the waiting room, their cacophony of moans, growls, and yowls—each one of my cats, upon hearing their siblings' anguished cries, louder than if they'd been there individually—drowning out the tweets, purrs, yips, and yelps of the semi-full room's other patients. Their owners gazed at me—sitting there alone, taking up three chairs, cat carriers surrounding me like a pillow fort—and then down toward my bare ring finger with an air of bemusement and pity. *How is it even possible,* I imagined them thinking, *that some lucky person hasn't already snatched up this gem?* I felt a childish, almost irresistible impulse to cry out, *I do so too* have someone! *He just isn't with me right now, is all.*

I hadn't planned to be in that waiting room alone with my cats that day. But it was a day when nothing had gone as planned . . .

IN MY ORIGINAL BLUEPRINT for that afternoon, Laurence was supposed to be there with me. The only reason I'd booked all three cats for their annuals on the same day was because we'd agreed that, under the circumstances, it was a necessity—one that Laurence would help me execute.

I had moved, a month earlier, into the apartment where Laurence had lived for seventeen years. He was in possession of the Manhattan equivalent of the Holy Grail, the kind of thing you heard urban legends about, but never expected to see in your own real life: a rent-controlled, three-bedroom, two-bathroom apartment *with a terrace,* in a Midtown doorman high-rise, for a three-figure monthly rent. (Eight years later, our unit would phase out of rent control and the rent would skyrocket to six thousand a month—at which point Laurence and I made a beeline for Jersey City.)

Technically it was a "no pets" building, but the rent was too insanely good not to at least try to make it work. On my move-in day, we'd tipped the super for use of the freight elevator (located in the rear of the building), and I'd managed to sneak in the three cat carriers among my boxes and suitcases without having to worry about the scrutiny of the lobby staff.

Nevertheless, the possibility of discovery was an ongoing concern. I had some savings, and Laurence—having lived so inexpensively for so long—had a lot more. We had more than enough between us, in other words, to finance a hasty move if we were suddenly evicted for illicit cat possession. And Laurence, who'd been there far longer than all but a handful of the other tenants, knew and was liked by everyone who worked in the building. Various maintenance men had come and gone over the past few weeks, and—while we'd locked the cats in a bedroom, not wanting to be *too* obvious—the clearly audible sound of three outraged felines, who were unused to being restrained, had passed unremarked. The maintenance guys had simply made whatever repairs they'd come to make, accepted our cash tip when they were finished, and left without comment.

Still, it seemed wise not to flaunt the cats where flaunting was avoidable. So when the time for their annual exams rolled around, I booked a single three-cat appointment with a new vet (our old vet now being a forty-minute, twenty-dollar crosstown cab ride away), figuring it made more sense for Laurence and me to hustle the three cats quickly through the lobby and past the doorman in one straight shot, rather than trying to do so on three separate occasions. Plus, we reasoned, our new doctor might as well meet them all at once.

But, as the saying goes, man plans and God laughs. At the last minute, Laurence, who was a film journalist with *Variety* at the time, got assigned to cover the press junket for the new *Zorro* movie. He'd have to attend a private screening of the film uptown, following which he'd head for a suite at the Waldorf Astoria to sit for a roundtable discussion with one of the principals—just Laurence, three other reporters, and Catherine Zeta-Jones, hanging out to talk about whatever movie stars and movie reporters talk about when they get together.

"So what you're telling me," I said to Laurence, "is that you want me to lug all three cats to the vet's office *by myself*, so you can spend the afternoon with Catherine Zeta-Jones."

"It sounds bad when you put it that way," Laurence admitted.

We briefly considered changing the appointment, but it wasn't as if I'd never managed on my own to get all three of them to the vet at once. Granted, the last time had been four years ago, when I'd brought the cats to our Miami vet to get their airline travel certificates so they could ride with me in the plane's cabin during our move to New York. And things had been different back then in certain crucial ways, although I didn't stop to think about that before agreeing to send Laurence off to Catherine Zeta-Jones and go it alone. I'd been living in a pet-friendly apartment building, for one thing. And for another, I'd had my own car.

Neither of those was the case now.

The first hurdle was clearing the lobby of our building without arousing the doorman's suspicions. It was early fall—not yet true coat weather, but not the kind of broiling-hot day that would make coat-wearing overly suspicious. The original plan had been for Laurence to hide Vashti and Scarlett's carriers under his coat, and for me to carry Homer under my own, until we got outside.

Now I had to find outerwear that could effectively hide three cat carriers on its own. I had a vintage swing-coat of my grandmother's, made in the '60s, that I thought might do the trick. Its great swath of cherry-red fabric fell from a high leopard-print collar into a wide, beltless balloon, which Laurence claimed made me look like Emma Peel from *The Avengers* whenever I wore it.

Checking myself out in the hall mirror before I left—with Scarlett's carrier slung over one shoulder under the coat, Vashti's over the other, and Homer's clutched in my hands in front of me beneath the coat's girth—I didn't look a bit like Emma Peel. I looked armless and startlingly obese, my legs descending beneath the coat's knee-length hem like two toothpicks supporting a bowling ball.

Actually, I assured myself, the bowling-ball comparison wasn't entirely fair. Bowling balls don't meow, after all, whereas a raucous and colorful string of feline oaths was already emerging from beneath my coat's copious folds. Homer, in particular, was swearing up a storm as he loudly—and repeatedly—let me know exactly what he thought of this nonsense.

Well, I thought, *at least I'm not conspicuous.*

"Be cool, you guys," I pleaded with the cats, speaking down to them through the coat's high collar as I emerged from the elevator into the lobby. The sound of cars whizzing by on Second Avenue from beyond the building's front doors momentarily silenced them, for which I was infinitely grateful. I could walk neither well nor quickly, laden down as I was beneath my heavy coat and nearly thirty pounds of catflesh, so I did a sort of quick-time waddle past the doorman's desk.

The doorman regarded me quizzically for a moment before his face broke out into a broad smile. "Look at you!" he exclaimed heartily. "Congratulations!" I had no idea what he was talking about, as he continued to beam at me, until he added, "When are you due?"

Nothing makes a woman feel better than being mistaken for pregnant when she's not. But I didn't know how much longer my cats would remain silent, and I certainly wasn't looking to prolong the conversation. So I said, rather lamely, "No sooner than I have to be" (even I wasn't sure what that meant), and waddled even faster toward the lobby's front door.

"Oh, no—allow me," the doorman insisted, racing from behind his desk to open the door for me, then plunging himself into the gray, overcast afternoon and the whirl of Second Avenue traffic to flag down a cab. I waited until I could see he was safely back inside and out of eyeshot—pausing to give me a friendly goodbye wave as he disappeared back through the front door—before I opened my coat and began arranging the carriers on the cab's backseat.

"It's like a clown car in there," the cabbie observed cheerfully, as one cat after another emerged from the inner recesses of my outerwear.

I hadn't anticipated finding myself in the back of a cab with such speed and ease, and my relief was great enough that I let the comment go by. "We're going straight down Second Avenue," I told the cabbie. Pulling Homer's carrier onto my lap and checking that Scarlett's and Vashti's were still securely closed, I leaned back and closed my eyes. The hardest part was over.

🐾 🐾

IN THE FLUSTERED HASTE to get out of the apartment, I hadn't noted the exact address of our new veterinary clinic. But a newly launched web mapping service called Google Maps had revealed St. Mark's Veterinary Hospital to be on the northwest corner of St. Mark's Place (another name for Eighth Street) and First

A   v   -
enue.

The East Village, as the area was known, was an older, pre-skyscraper section of Manhattan, and St. Mark's Place had once been the flashpoint of New York's counterculture. Although slowly gentrifying, it still retained something of its bohemian charm and was colorful and crowded as a Moroccan bazaar, albeit one that had been taken over by hippies, artists, and hawkers of tourist tchotchkes. There were also plenty of increasingly expensive apartments in the East Village's aging brownstones and tenements, at least some of which, presumably, housed conscientious pet custodians. And, of all the veterinary practices within a reasonable distance of the cats' and my new home, St. Mark's Vet seemed the most beloved by its clientele, judging by online reviews.

Laurence and I lived at Twenty-Eighth and Second. We could make it down to St. Mark's Place in about half an hour on foot, and even in the stop-and-go traffic on Second, I didn't think it would be more than a fifteen-minute ride. Still, I'd left home at 1:45 p.m. for our 2:30 p.m. appointment, assuming it would take me longer to find a cab than it ultimately had, and also because a certain compulsiveness when it came to punctuality had been baked into my DNA. Even when going to her nail salon, a three-minute drive from her house, my mother down in Florida would first check rain forecasts, traffic reports, construction updates, the air level in the tires of her car, the very wind velocity for all I knew—and then still leave a half-hour early because "You never know *what's* going to happen with all the idiots driving around Miami."

We crept along for about ten blocks, the cabbie hitting the brakes hard every minute or so as the cars in front of us ground to a halt. Every time the cab stopped, a cat would start to wail, but only one at a time, as if they'd agreed upon a particular sequence beforehand. (I found this fascinating and tried to figure it out—were they going oldest to youngest? largest to smallest?—but couldn't detect a pattern.) I'd gotten so used to the rhythm of go/stop/cat cry, go/stop/cat cry that—when I heard a dull crunch of metal and was suddenly flung forward against the plastic divider separating the front seat of the cab from the back, then backward against the backseat headrest—I didn't register at first that anything odder than a particularly hard slam of the brakes had occurred. Then I realized that I had a painful lump blossoming on my forehead, and that Scarlett's and Vashti's carriers had lurched forward and were now wedged between the divider and the edge of the back seat. Homer's, fortunately, was still safely in my lap.

A quick check revealed all three cats to be unharmed. Nevertheless, the immediate roar of their caterwauling nearly drowned out the cabbie's loud curses as he threw the car into park, turned on his hazard lights, and flung open the driver's side door, leaping out to confront the driver who'd rear-ended us. It was difficult for the cats to make themselves heard over the angry blare of horns that rose from the cars behind us. But my cats were pros. They managed.

Shhhhhhh . . . it's okay . . . everything's going to be oooooookay . . . I murmured in the most soothing voice I could muster. But my cats argued stridently and persuasively that it most definitely was *not* going to be okay; with Homer, who always did have the most expressive cat voice I'd ever heard, making a particularly compelling case. My only hope was that the damage would prove minor enough for us to continue on our way. That hope was dashed, however, as the cabbie returned to dig out his cell phone from the front seat. "I'm calling the cops," he told me. "You should probably go find another cab."

I was momentarily nonplussed, possessed by the swift, wholly irrational feeling that I would rather do anything—literally, *anything*—than get out of that cab, shoulder my three cats, and go looking for another ride. "Don't you need me to stay and be a witness for the police report or something?"

The cabbie gave me a look that eloquently expressed his rapidly diminishing opinion of my intelligence. "Did you *see* anything?"

"Well . . . no."

"Just go. And don't worry about the fare," he added (rather graciously, all things considered) as I opened my purse to dig around for my wallet.

Heaving a sigh, I hoisted Scarlett's and Vashti's carriers over the shoulders of my unbuttoned coat and cradled Homer's in my arms in front of me, stepping out into the gray day and walking along the sidewalk backward as I scanned Second Avenue for another available cab. Even Vashti—patient, squeaky-voiced Vashti—had been pushed beyond endurance, lowing her misery to an indifferent universe in deep, wrenching tones. Their complaints only rose in volume as I felt first one raindrop, then a second splash onto the top of my head before the clouds that had been piling up all day in an ever-angrier blue-black bruise finally opened, and it started to rain in earnest.

Of *course* it started to rain.

Ducking under an awning, I divested myself of cats and coat so that I could reassemble everything with all three carriers once again secured beneath the coat's folds, this time to protect them from the deluge. In the process, I attracted lively interest from the patrons of the bakery behind me, whose awning I was temporarily sheltering beneath. As they comfortably sipped their coffee and ate their scones and pointed me out to companions in backward-facing chairs who swiveled around for a better view, I had an urge to wave my arms around and holler, *LOOK AT ME, EVERYBODY! LOOK AT THE CRAAAAAAAZY CAT LADY! TWO BITS A GANDER!* But I restrained myself and merely sighed again, dashing back out into the rain once the cats were settled. Carrying Homer beneath my coat with both hands meant I didn't have one free to make use of the fold-up umbrella in my purse, but by then I was already so thoroughly soaked that it hardly seemed to matter.

I tottered along awkwardly for about three blocks without seeing a single available taxi. I watched as one occupied cab after another crawled by, muttering darkly under my breath about the callous insensitivity of a city where not *one* person was willing to stop and split their fare with a fake-pregnant lady stuck in the rain. My damp hair plastered itself against my face, and I thought ruefully of the high and wild "Jew-fro" I was sure to have once it was dry again. The cats, who were now putting up an active revolt from within their carriers, felt decidedly heavier than when I'd first started out—and, despite the rain and early-autumn coolness, I perspired heavily beneath my coat. The ache in my shoulders intensified as the cats twisted and turned in their confines, shifting their weight unevenly from front to back and side to side as they sought in vain for an escape. By all rights, on a rainy day like this one, they should have been warm and dry at home, snoozing blissfully in front of the heater. I can only assume they thought I'd woken up that morning possessed of a perverse and irresistible desire to ruin their lives and that, after much consideration, I'd finally hit upon the perfect plan for doing so.

Water was filling up inside my fashionable ankle boots ("fashionable" here should be read as shorthand for "impractical for walking in the rain"), and I was just about to dash under another awning and wait out the downpour, our scheduled appointment be damned, when a battered Lincoln Town Car that had seen better days—very obviously a gypsy cab—pulled up alongside me. The driver rolled down his window and shouted, "You headed downtown?"

In the days before Uber, gypsy cabs were basically random guys with Town Cars who cruised around the city looking for (illegal) fares among the sidewalk downtrodden—people who either weren't savvy enough to avoid gypsy cabs or who lacked better options. I avoided gypsy cabs on general principle. In the first place, their fares were almost always outrageous (see above re: naïve and desperate clientele). And, in the second place, I had a long-standing wariness—impressed upon me since childhood—of getting into cars with strange men.

But there I was, standing in the middle of a downpour with three livid cats—mad as hell and hot as radiators—stashed beneath the sopping and sweaty coat I now fully intended to burn when I finally got back home. I looked first at the mustachioed driver, and then at the bobble-headed cat statue that bounced merrily on his dashboard. I think it may have mesmerized me. *Go ahead,* it seemed to whisper. *What else are you going to do?*

I took a step closer to the car. "How much to go to Eighth Street and First?"

"Twenty dollars," the driver said immediately.

"*Twenty dollars?*" I screeched. "To go *ten* blocks? That's crazy!" The driver didn't even bother responding. I was in a fix, and we both knew it. I reluctantly conceded, "All right," opened the door to the backseat, and once again started unpacking my cats from beneath my coat.

"Wait, you've got *animals* in there?" the driver protested. "I don't want them messing up my car."

The Town Car's gray interior had a reek of cheap air freshener unsuccessfully masking onions, and had been inexpertly patched in numerous places with fraying electrical tape. Was he kidding? Biting back a sharp retort, however, I observed wearily, "They're in carriers. They won't mess anything up. I promise."

"It'll be an extra ten dollars," the driver informed me.

"Fine, *whatever*." I loaded the cats into the car and flung myself in behind them, imagining the coronary Laurence would have if he knew I was preparing to hand over thirty dollars to a gypsy-cab driver to travel a distance of only ten blocks. "Just get us to Eighth and First."

I expected the oniony stench—never a favorite with my felines—to provoke a fresh round of complaints. But the cats had apparently entered into a state of trauma-induced catatonia and were silent. The only sound to be heard, aside from the pounding Middle Eastern electronica coming from the car radio—which seemed to pulsate in tempo with the lump on my forehead—was the ringing of my cell phone from within my purse. Laurence had just gotten out of his movie and was awaiting the arrival of Catherine Zeta-Jones.

"How's it going? Are you at the vet's office yet?"

"Not yet. We hit a few snags," I told him. "How's it going there?"

"It's great," Laurence said cheerfully. "I just heard someone say they're bringing in sandwiches from Carnegie Deli."

"Lucky you," I replied wistfully, and heard a faint corroborating rumble from the vicinity of my stomach.

"I can bring a sandwich home for you," Laurence offered.

Traffic had eased considerably once we'd gotten past Fourteenth Street, and the Town Car was now closing in on Ninth. "That sounds good," I told him. "I'll see you at home."

"See you at home," he said.

The downpour had stopped by the time we reached the corner of Eighth and First. Gathering the folds of my wet coat around me, I felt reinvigorated at the prospect of my long, painful journey to the vet's office having finally reached its conclusion. Even handing over the staggering thirty-dollar fare (*Don't you dare tip him*, I could hear Laurence admonish) wasn't as onerous as I'd thought it would be. "Here we go, guys," I told the cats happily as I lifted their carriers for our short walk to the clinic. "Time to meet your new vet!"

TWENTY MINUTES LATER, WE were now officially five minutes late for our appointment—and apparently no closer to St. Mark's Veterinary Hospital than we'd been when we'd first left home nearly an hour ago.

I'd gotten out of the car with my cats at the corner of Eighth and First, and hadn't seen anything remotely resembling an animal hospital among the rainbow of storefronts and restaurants that dotted this stretch of St. Mark's Place. Reassuring myself, with the remembered vision of what Google Maps had shown me, that it was probably only a little farther down, I'd hobbled along the street as best I could in my water-stiffened boots, which were now raising blisters on my ankles, and my sopping-wet coat—and with what felt like a permanent hunch forming in my upper back as I bore the weight of three wretched cats who seemed, through sheer spite, to have somehow willed themselves into being heavier than they actually were.

Having resumed their insistent wailing, they had shifted their tone from plaintive and cajoling (*Please, pleeeeeeeease, let us out, mommy . . .*) to distinctly hostile (*Up yours, lady!*). Scarlett, my "surly girl" who could sound downright mean-spirited when she had a mind to, kept up a continuous, cantankerous, and guttural stream of personal insults that would undoubtedly be unprintable if translated from feline to human. "Stop *yelling* at me, Scarlett!" I kept shouting. "I can't *think!*" That was when I wasn't hollering at my fellow pedestrians, who persistently bumped into me—a limping hunchback smothered in cats—as a not-so-gentle reminder that my shuffling pace was slowing down the flow of traffic. "Hey!" I heard myself snarl at their retreating backs. "I'm walking here! *I'm walking here!*" I felt a sudden stab of sympathy for those people you saw from time to time, wandering the streets of New York alone, hands balled into fists as they raged and raved at nobody in particular. Maybe they all had grousing cats stuffed beneath their coats, too.

I peered up at every sign and into every doorway that I passed as I waddled up Eighth Street. By the time I made it all the way to Second Avenue—with Gem Spa (an ancient newsstand and home of the world's best egg cream) and Love Saves the Day (my all-time favorite vintage store) swimming before my bleary eyes—I knew I'd overshot the mark.

The lump on my forehead throbbed dully. It occurred to me that if I hadn't possibly concussed myself earlier when the cab was rear-ended, I would've already come up with the bright idea of digging out my cell phone and calling Information for the exact address. Setting Homer's carrier on the ground to free up my hands and clutching it firmly between my ankles (raised in Miami during the snatch-and-grab '80s, I maintained an irrational and unshakeable belief that any improperly secured bag would be stolen instantly), I swung my handbag around from its perch on my shoulder just above Scarlett's carrier and began pawing through it. I'd deliberately chosen a small bag when I'd left the house, to minimize the weight I'd be carrying around that afternoon. It didn't take more than a few seconds, therefore, to discover that my phone was nowhere to be found.

I frantically dug through all my pockets and then, moving off to the edge of the sidewalk farthest from the street, I squatted on the ground, settled all three carriers beside me, and actually emptied the contents of my purse and pockets onto the pavement. The brief glimpse I caught, in my compact mirror, of my bird's-nest hair and sweaty, makeup-streaked face was both horrifying and revelatory. Along with my scratched-up hands (from my earlier efforts to get Homer into his carrier), swollen ankles, lumpy forehead, bedraggled coat, and warped shoes, plus the effluvia from the inside of my purse spread out before me as I snatched at lipsticks and bits of paper that attempted to roll away, and my array of cranky cats—whose dour expressions made it clear that they'd rather be anywhere in the world than stuck with *this* crazy lady—my *Whatever Happened to Baby Jane?* hair and face probably explained why one well-dressed woman, barely breaking stride, went so far as to chuck a dollar bill in my direction as she strode past.

I had officially been downgraded from pedestrian to panhandler.

Still squatting on the sidewalk, I buried my face in my hands and took a deep breath—which only prompted a fresh volley of bills and loose change from passersby. A busker a few feet away glared at me, and I responded with a gesture that I hoped conveyed (among other things) that if he wanted the cash so badly, he should come and get it. *Get up,* I commanded myself. It was very clear by now that I'd left my phone in the backseat of the gypsy cab after Laurence's phone call. With no phone and dwindling cash, it still made more sense for me to try to find the vet's office—which, surely, I must be closing in on!—than to return home. I'd have to walk back to First Avenue, anyway, to catch a cab or bus that was going in the right direction to get us to our apartment. My best plan, therefore, was to ask someone for directions. One of the shopkeepers or employees along this stretch of St. Mark's Place would undoubtedly be able to tell me where St. Mark's Vet was located. Accordingly, I scooped my belongings back into my purse and hoisted my cats once again.

It seemed, however, that nobody could help me. As I limped my way back down Eighth Street, I got blank stares from the dazed proprietors of the numerous head shops I ducked into; the sidewalk vendors selling postcards and knickknacks; the girl with shocking pink hair, a pierced lip, and tattooed arms at punk-rock mecca Trash and Vaudeville; the sad day-drinkers at Holiday Cocktail Lounge. I was admonished, *You can't bring animals in here!* in a diverse array of languages at a taqueria, a stand-up pizza counter, a falafel joint, and a take-out dumpling place. Each time the aroma of cooking food hit Homer's nostrils, he began pinging wildly at the sides of his carrier, until it felt like I was trying to hold onto a super-sized container of Jiffy Pop.

It wasn't until I'd retraced my steps all the way back to the corner of Eighth and First, and poked my head into Theatre 80, that I found salvation. Laurence and I had attended many performances at the Off-Broadway theater and had struck up conversations along the way with Lorcan Otway, the old-school Quaker (I'd thought he might be Amish when I first met him, because of the way he dressed) whose family had owned the place for decades. Silently offering me a glass of water from the lobby bar when I entered, and generously refraining from any remarks on my appearance, Lorcan removed his wide-brimmed, black-felt hat to rub his head in contemplation as I put my question to him. "Oh, yeah—St. Mark's Vet," he finally said. "They moved over to Ninth Street about a year ago." At seeing my shoulders slump (while I inwardly cursed Google Maps and its outdated information), Lorcan added kindly, "They're right at the corner of Ninth and First. You're practically there already."

I was so ecstatic upon seeing the brightly painted sign that read St. Mark's Veterinary Hospital almost immediately upon rounding the corner of Ninth and First that I barely minded when, as I tried to navigate the narrow metal staircase leading down to the basement-level entry, the warped and rain-soaked soles of my boots slid out from beneath me. I landed flat on my backside on a hard metal step, adding a bruise on my coccyx to the one on my forehead. Fortunately, I noted as I unsteadily rose back to my feet, I hadn't dropped or fallen on any of the cats.

The landing at the bottom of the stairs was a tight space, and I had to turn and twist for a good ten seconds before finally finding an angle that would allow me to both open the front door and squeeze through with my three carriers. When the sunny receptionist chirpily informed me that I'd missed my appointment and might have to wait awhile, I didn't bat an eyelash. I was so happy to be there—*at last! at last!*—and safely beyond the reach of sudden cloudbursts or hostile pedestrians that I was tempted to leap over the counter and kiss her on the mouth.

Instead of doing that, however, I asked permission to use the office phone to call my cell. It was answered by the gypsy-cab driver, who agreed to drive over and return it to me—for another twenty dollars.

PERHAPS THE GREATEST IRONY of that day was that the exams themselves—the insertion of needles and rectal thermometers, the prying back of reluctant lips to check teeth and gums—turned out to be the high point. Or Vashti's and Scarlett's exams were, at any rate. After the hour spent in the waiting room with my three furious felines, the doctor's kind patience was a balm on my frayed nerves, if not my cats'. Things went swimmingly until it was Homer's turn on the exam table. A vet tech chose the moment that Homer was finally released from his carrier to enter our exam room and, upon detecting the change in the air currents when the door opened, Homer—quick as a light beam—leapt down from the high metal table and streaked through the partially opened door in a mad dash for freedom.

You'd think it would be easy enough to catch a five-pound blind cat in an enclosed space that was entirely unfamiliar to him. And you would be wrong. Homer raced down the long hallway of exam rooms and out into the waiting area, sure-footed as if he had a blueprint of the building sketched in his head. My own bruised and battered body wasn't nearly so nimble as I lurched after him. Darting perilously close to the snout of a startled black Lab before wheeling around and changing course, Homer propelled himself into a storage closet whose door had been left ajar. "Please, Homer," I begged, as Homer sat on his haunches on a shelf just above my head, wholly intractable and entirely confident in the advantage over me that height gave him. "Please come down and get your exam like a good boy, so we can all go home."

Normally, Homer would do anything I asked (other than getting into his carrier, that is) if I used the right tone of voice. But I hadn't built up much in the way of credibility over the course of that long day, and Homer wasn't buying it. *No!* he seemed to say. *And you can't make me!* I felt absurdly triumphant when I finally located a small stepladder in a corner of the storage closet. I might not have been able to outwit any of the other obstacles the day had thrown at me, but I could still outsmart my cat. Cocking one black ear in my direction and tilting his head to the side as he tried to figure out what I was up to, Homer put up only token resistance as I ascended the stepladder and pulled him from his perch. The firmness of my grip on the scruff of his neck didn't leave room for argument.

I cradled him in my arms for a moment before exiting the storage closet—an unexpected oasis of calm in our chaotic day. There had never been a day so long and so bad that holding one of my cats close couldn't make it at least a little better. Pressing my cheek to the top of Homer's head and breathing in the familiar cinnamon-and-milk smell of his neck (I don't know how Homer always managed to smell like cookies, but he did, and it was awesome), I could feel the knots in my shoulders start to unloosen. "We're still friends," I whispered in Homer's ear, "aren't we?" He appeared to consider this for a moment before mashing his entire face into the palm of my hand, our usual gesture of reconciliation. I dropped a kiss onto the top of his head, and the two of us returned to the exam room.

By the time we emerged from the vet's office it was rush hour, which would have made finding a cab nearly impossible even if—having already spent fifty dollars on the gypsy cab and the return of my cell phone—I'd had the cash to pay for one. The bus was our only alternative. The late-afternoon sun had made a belated appearance after all the rain, and it was considerably warmer out than it had been when I'd left the apartment hours ago. Still, I didn't have the energy to take off my coat as I slowly toted the cats up to the bus stop on Eleventh and First. *Like it matters how much sweatier I get at this point,* I thought.

The bus was jam-packed with rush-hour commuters when we finally boarded, and an elderly woman, upon seeing how laden down with cats I was, immediately rose to offer me her seat. "*Please* don't," I insisted, raising the arm carrying Scarlett to grasp one of the straps hanging above my head. Vashti continued to dangle from my other shoulder, and I settled Homer on the floor of the bus between my feet. Gesturing to the carriers and the sardine-can crowd around us, I added, "I wouldn't have any room to put all three of them down, anyway."

The woman beamed first at me, as the bus lurched forward, and then at the cats through the mesh of their carriers. She reached up to rub gently at the front of Scarlett's, and I could feel Scarlett retreating as far back into her carrier as she could, reluctant as always to engage in any unnecessary human contact. "I have three of my own," the woman confided. "Where are the four of you coming from?"

"The vet's office," I replied.

"Ah! I try to never bring my three in all together. It's hard getting around New York with three cats. Unless," she smiled up at me again, "I bring my husband to help out. You should find someone to come with you next time."

"I think you're probably right about that," I agreed ruefully.

The bus let us off at the corner of Twenty-Eighth and First, and I was so grateful to finally—finally!—be so close to home that I nearly wept. Halfway between First and Second, I paused under the awning of a medical building to once again assemble the cats under my coat, in anticipation of the return trip through my apartment building's lobby. The doormen had changed shifts by then, and the evening doorman barely glanced up at me—much less congratulated me on my "pregnancy"—as I waddled my way past the front desk.

The sound of the radio drifting toward the elevator through our apartment door, once I reached our floor, let me know that Laurence had beaten me home. Undoubtedly, he would be fresh as a daisy after a day spent being feted at the Waldorf Astoria uptown. After my own afternoon trudging around downtown, I knew I was anything but. Nevertheless, the prospect of sympathy—and a

Carnegie Deli sandwich—waiting for me inside went at least part of the way toward erasing the day's awfulness.

The first thing I did upon entering the apartment and closing the door behind me was to strip off my coat and hurl it into a corner, then kneel to release the cats from the confines of their carriers. Our entry hallway opened into both the living room and the kitchen, and I headed directly for the kitchen cabinet where I kept the cat treats. I distributed them with a free hand, feeling that my cats also deserved some recompense for the miserable afternoon we'd all had. A few cursory brushes of backsides and tails against my shins let me know that I would be forgiven—eventually.

Upon hearing the kitchen cabinet open and close, Laurence called out, "You home?"

"I just walked in," I called back. "How'd it go?"

I heard the sound of Laurence rising from the couch. "It was great! Catherine Zeta-Jones was unbelievable. She..." Having closed the short distance between living room and kitchen and drawn near enough to take in my appearance for the first time, Laurence's voice trailed off and he whistled softly. "Yikes," he said. "Bad day?"

"Don't ask."

Laurence moved closer. "What happened here?" he asked, gently brushing a finger against the purple lump on my forehead.

I attempted a smile. "Nothing a good sandwich can't fix," I replied lightly.

Laurence opened the refrigerator and withdrew a paper bag. "Chopped liver for you," he said, "and pastrami for me."

I retreated to the bathroom and, bending over the sink, tried to wash as much of the day's grime as possible from my face and hands. I heard Laurence gathering plates and napkins as I dried off with a hand towel, and we reconvened on the living room couch.

The cats and I hadn't been living with Laurence for very long at that point, but Vashti had already learned that he (unlike mom) could be counted on to slip a few tidbits her way at mealtimes, and had accordingly positioned herself on the floor close to his feet. Homer, who adored deli meats and could put away an astonishing amount of food for such a small cat, sat on the couch between

Laurence and me, his face turned toward Laurence in hopeful anticipation. After only a few weeks, he'd learned from Vashti that the longstanding rule in our home against feeding table scraps to cats was in the process of being rewritten.

Only Scarlett sat aloof, perched across from us on the coffee table with disdain plainly written on her face. She had never been a fan of human food, and thus her affections couldn't be bought as easily as Vashti's and Homer's were. To Scarlett's way of thinking, anyone living in our home who wasn't me was just another cat—and Laurence was nothing more than the largest and most annoying of all the new cats I'd foisted upon her over the years. As the self-appointed leader and maintainer of discipline within our feline ranks, Scarlett had attempted to teach Laurence his proper place in the hierarchy with a peremptory swipe of her claws whenever he brushed too closely against her while passing in the halls. Puzzlingly, however, Laurence hadn't learned to defer to her as quickly as the other two cats had. Her deep disapproval now as Vashti and Homer lowered themselves and actually *begged* this interloper for a few crumbs from his plate was nearly palpable.

"So, you didn't finish telling me how it went," I said to Laurence. "What was Catherine Zeta-Jones like?"

"She was amazing!" He tore open a packet of mustard and applied it to his rye bread, Vashti and Homer at rapt attention as he did so. "I had such a great time talking with her! She really has that movie-star *thing*."

Laurence met and interviewed celebrities on a fairly regular basis—it was a part of his job description—and it was unusual for him to sound so animated about any one of them in particular. And yet, he still wasn't finished waxing lyrical on the subject of Ms. Zeta-Jones's many charms. "When she walks into a room, you *have* to look at her," he enthused. "She just *glows,* you know?"

A quick glimpse in the bathroom mirror as I'd washed earlier up had revealed how disheveled I'd become over the course of the day: With the puddled makeup still caked around my eyes—I'd done my best to wipe it away but I knew that only a long shower would do the job fully—I looked like an aging raccoon. My hair was a fright wig straight out of one of the witches' scenes in *Macbeth*.

The wreckage of my appearance could have been described in any number of ways, but "glowing" with "that movie-star *thing*" was certainly not among them.

I'll bet Catherine Zeta-Jones has somebody to take her *cats to the vet for her,* I thought sourly as I bit into my own sandwich—not knowing or caring whether Catherine Zeta-Jones even had cats. *I'll bet she has cat butlers or cat valets, or some other dumb thing only rich movie stars have. I'll bet if Catherine Zeta-Jones does go the vet's office, she probably comes back looking like a million freaking dollars.* AND WHAT KIND OF STUPID NAME IS "ZETA-JONES" ANYWAY?

I knew I was being at least a little childish. Obviously, Laurence hadn't intended to draw comparisons. But I couldn't help the tenor of my thoughts, which I struggled to keep from revealing themselves on my face.

Laurence was sitting sideways on the couch, partially turned to face me. He held his still-untasted sandwich loosely in one hand—the hand closest to the coffee table—and, in his enthusiasm, gestured with it as he spoke. "She's really funny, too." The sandwich in Laurence's hand moved nearer to Scarlett's nose, which was wrinkling with distaste. "So many of them have nothing interesting to say for themselves." The pastrami and rye waved even closer to Scarlett's increasingly agitated face. "But she—" With one slight, but fatal, additional motion, the sandwich drew close enough to Scarlett to brush her whiskers.

It was the last straw in a day that had, I was forced to acknowledge, been as unpleasant for Scarlett as it was for me. I'll never know if she had drawn any connection between Laurence's last-minute absence that day and how badly our afternoon had gone—or if she was able to tell from my expression what my own feelings toward Laurence were as I listened to him rhapsodize about Catherine Zeta-Jones. Regardless, this final insult was clearly too much for her to bear. With a loud hiss, Scarlett raised a front paw into the air—and, before I could stop her, brought it down in an angry swipe at Laurence's sandwich, which tumbled from his incautious hand and landed with a *splat!* on the floor.

In a flash, Homer leapt nimbly from the couch and was on top of the remnants of Laurence's meal, nosing assiduously through its wreckage for bits of pastrami that hadn't been contaminated by mustard.

"Hey!" Laurence's eyes turned to Scarlett in astonishment, then down toward the ruined pile of meat and bread on the ground. By now, Vashti had joined Homer and was gleefully helping herself, either not knowing that Laurence hadn't intended to give it to her, or else, in her excitement, not caring. It was difficult to tell which was stronger in Laurence's voice, anger or betrayal, as he said, "What was *that* for?"

I couldn't help myself—I burst out laughing. I laughed until tears ran from my eyes to blend with the black rings of eyeliner and mascara I knew were still there. "You can have half of my chopped liver, if you want," I finally offered, when I was able to catch my breath.

Scarlett let out a harrumph-y sniff, the gray-and-black tabby-striped fur of her back twitching rapidly, as she jumped down from the coffee table. With baleful eyes she looked back at Laurence, who was still gazing with dismay at what was left of his sandwich, before coldly stalking off toward the bedroom.

"What's her problem?" Laurence asked again—and it's possible that, in that moment, Scarlett and I had the same thought:

Why don't you go ask Catherine Zeta-Jones.

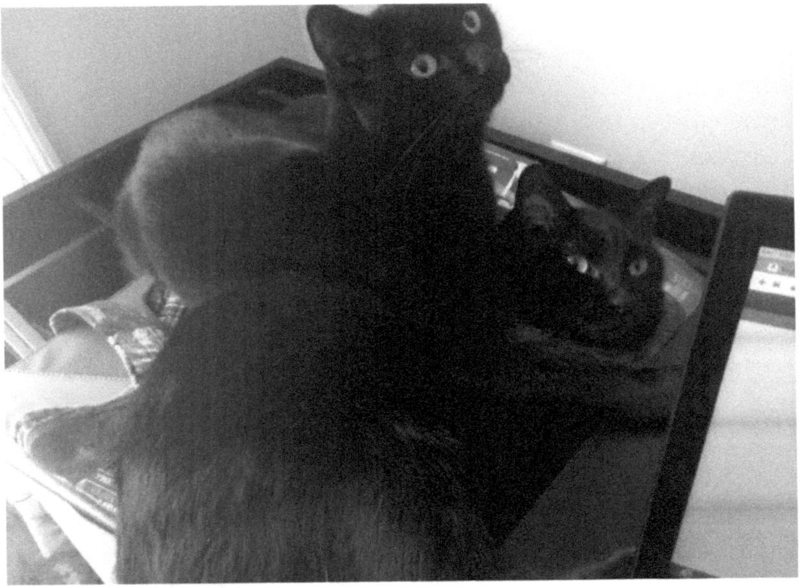

The Infestation

1. The Bowl Boy

Laurence and I uncovered an infestation of moths in our closets and drawers a few weeks ago. It was the kind of thing I thought only happened to people in sitcoms and movies—having never personally known anyone with a moth-ridden house in real life. Turns out, it *does* happen in real life. When I first started finding holes in the cashmere sweaters I was prepping for summer storage, I blamed the cats—Fanny, in particular, who dearly loves sleeping on articles of my clothing, especially when that clothing is made of cashmere or angora (Fanny having very posh tastes). I've occasionally observed her remorselessly "making biscuits" on said clothing—her claws at full extension—preparatory to lying down. It seemed like a plausible theory.

But when I then found identical holes in T-shirts, sweatshirts, silk blouses, pajamas, socks, workout togs, and all manner of other clothing that neither Fanny nor Clayton had access to, I began to doubt the cats' guilt. And when I finally noticed two teeny-tiny moths, perched upside down on the bedroom ceiling above my head, I knew I'd found my culprits.

Tearfully, I consigned a large pile of expensive cashmere sweaters—accumulated over some fifteen years—to the trash, the holes in them so numerous that no amount of clever crocheting could have salvaged them. I walked from the bedroom closet to Laurence's home office, right next door to our bedroom, cradling in my arms the moth-eaten corpse of a much-beloved cranberry cowl-neck as tenderly as if it were the bullet-riddled body of a comrade fallen in battle. Throwing it across the desk where Laurence was working, I informed him of the moth-y new development in our lives. "We must kill them," I announced. My voice quavered with the intensity of my desire for vengeance, and I struck my fist on Laurence's desk for dramatic emphasis. "*We must kill them with fire!*"

The only ones who seemed pleased at this turn of events were the cats. My manic tear through our closets and drawers, after I'd discovered the first moth holes, had sent airborne perhaps another half-dozen moths who'd been disturbed from the cool, dark comfort of their hiding places. Small as they were, their frantic, looping cartwheels in the air around us made the catching of them a delightfully tantalizing prospect for Fanny and Clayton.

Poor, stocky Clayton, who has only one hind leg, is a mediocre jumper at best, and most of the moths evaded him easily enough. But his littermate, Fanny—slender and leanly muscled—is our resident jock. Able to leap from a starting point on the ground to the height of my hairline, with as much dazzling speed as if she were a black-furred bolt of lightning, Fanny was in her element as she made short work of one moth after another.

It's possible that Fanny is the actual sweetest cat in the world—a devoted lover who coos and cuddles and looks at me with her whole heart in her round, golden eyes—but she is, conversely, also the most murderous cat I've ever lived with. If Fanny has a bucket list, that list consists of only one item: to kill something worth killing before she shuffles off this mortal coil. Every spring, when the sparrows who nest in the eaves of our Jersey City brownstone push their fledglings down into the little patch of grass in front of our bay window, I have to lock Fanny in the upstairs bedroom for a couple of days, legitimately afraid that she might crack her skull from striking it repeatedly against the bay window's panes, so desperate is she to dispatch those temptingly plump and flightless baby birds as they hop around helplessly on the other side of the glass.

As a strictly indoor cat, Fanny never gets a chance at the birds or squirrels who seem to take a certain delight in taunting her from safe perches just outside our windows. And since I've never seen a rat or a mouse in any home I've shared with my cats—not even when we lived in Manhattan, dubbed "Worst Rat City in the

World" in 2014 by Animal Planet (presumably the rodents catch our home's cat smell and clear a wide berth)—Fanny is forced to expend her bloodlust on toy mice and whatever live insects manage to make their way indoors. The moths, therefore, were a bonanza for her.

They were, however, anything but a bonanza for me. I hadn't been kidding when I'd proclaimed, *"We must kill them with fire!"* A cursory check of Google revealed stories of people who'd been fighting moth infestations *for years*. I quickly outlined for Laurence what seemed to me an entirely rational plan of attack, involving roughly a metric ton of kerosene and a single lit match.

Cooler heads eventually prevailed, however. We ultimately embarked on a far more sensible course of action, purchasing dozens of boxes of mothballs, plastic zip-up storage bags, cedar hangers, two cans of repellant cedar spray, and another two cans of a pet-safe insecticide. We backed these up by emptying every single item out of every single closet and drawer and either putting them through three entire laundry cycles or, in the case of delicate fabrics, sending them out to the dry cleaner. Once everything had been cleaned, I then completed a thorough visual exam, sitting beneath a strong lamp with a magnifying glass in my hand as I pored over sweaters and wool dresses like a Talmudic scholar, searching for any telltale signs of moth larvae.

Having undertaken such an early and unexpectedly aggressive round of spring cleaning, Laurence and I decided we might as well give the entire house a thorough scrubbing from top to bottom and, in the process, dispose of all the superfluous *stuff* we'd accumulated over the years. Since we were, thanks to the lepidopteran pestilence visited upon us, getting rid of so many things we actually cared about, what was the point in hanging onto things we were indifferent to?

And here's where an old and familiar series of arguments began: Is it technically fair to call something "unused" if *we* never use it ourselves, but the *cats* use it all the time in some way other than its original intended purpose?

"You made me go out and buy that special cast-iron frying pan so you could make us omelets," I said to Laurence, "and we've still never had a single omelet in this house. The pan's been gathering dust on top of the kitchen cabinet for three years now."

"You really think we should get rid of it?" Laurence gestured across the room to indicate Fanny who, as if on cue, made a nimble leap from kitchen counter to cabinet top, then stepped neatly into the middle of the frying pan in question. "Someone might object."

It's true. Fanny has a fondness for high places—probably because the higher up she is, the less likely that Clayton will be able to pester her—and that frying pan had become her favorite kitchen napping spot. And I'll confess that, once I noticed how much she loved curling up there, I'd lined the pan with an old T-shirt, hating the thought of Fanny trying to make herself comfortable in a "bed" of cold, hard metal.

"What about that huge 'decorative bowl' you made us buy for the middle of the kitchen table?" Laurence suggested. "It doesn't *do* anything. It just sits there until we push it out of the way at dinnertime."

"No way!" I protested. "That's Clayton's favorite place to sleep when he's in the kitchen."

"He only ever comes down to the kitchen when we're not eating so he can bother Fanny," Laurence pointed out.

"Exactly," I replied. "And when he can't get to her, because she's on top of the cabinet in her frying pan, he goes to sleep in his bowl, and everybody's happy. I thought *you* thought it was so adorable of him," I added wistfully. "You always call him the 'bowl boy.'"

Moving through the house with an eye toward ridding ourselves of the unnecessary, it was astonishing to realize how many things had long since ceased to be of any practical value except insofar as the cats got some enjoyment out of them. For example, the gel pads I'd bought to support my wrists while I was typing, when I'd felt the earliest twinges of incipient carpal-tunnel syndrome (an occupational hazard for writers). Clayton, who likes to sleep next to me on my desk while I work, had immediately claimed them for his own, clawing at them until the gel oozed out to form sticky patches. This had rendered them unfit for my own use, obviously, but—once the sticky patches had attracted enough of Clayton's shed fur to make them more fuzzy than gummy—they made for ideal catnap pillows. I didn't really want to take those away from him, did I?

Then there was the recumbent exercise bike I'd installed in a corner of our bedroom, intending to ride it during the breaks I managed to snatch for reading a book while on writing deadlines. I'd ended up discovering, however, that I much preferred a couple of hours of dedicated gym time to twenty-minute increments here and there over the course of the day. Still, I'd been loath to try to resell it, because it was Clayton's favorite bedroom perch once we'd all turned in for the night. In any event, he'd "marked" the bike's faux-leather seat with his claws until it was so torn up that we probably couldn't have resold it even if we'd wanted to. There was plenty of room for it in the bedroom, so it was hard to see what harm we were doing by just letting it stay there.

We had empty shelves mounted on walls throughout the house, having planned once upon a time to display our knickknacks on them. But Fanny, with her love of high places, was apt to sleep on those shelves, and Clayton—when it came to the shelves he could actually climb up to—had a habit of pushing any knickknacks he encountered onto the floor. So the shelves remained empty, devoid of any justifiable use to our home's human inhabitants and making it look as if we were in a perpetual state of either moving in or moving out. Fanny was happy, though, which was the thing that really mattered.

There were two plush blankets that Laurence's sister had given us as holiday gifts last year—intending, I think, for Laurence and me to snuggle beneath them together while watching movies from the couch. But the cats adored all soft things, and the second we'd placed the blankets on the couch, Clayton and Fanny had sprawled out on them, rolling around ecstatically on their backs as they luxuriated in the plush texture. Now the blankets were thoroughly be-furred and wadded up on the ground, one in our third-floor bedroom and one in the book room on our middle floor.

"If anything's going to attract moths, those blankets will," Laurence said.

"Moths don't eat polyester," I replied.

Like all cats, Fanny and Clayton loved cardboard boxes more than just about anything. Accordingly, a few old shoeboxes had taken up a permanent residence on our living-room floor. "We can finally get rid of *those*—can't we?" Laurence suggested, pointing to two boxes that the cats happened to be sleeping in at that exact moment. As if they understood what we were saying, Clayton and Fanny looked up at us, anxious pleas for clemency written in four identical golden eyes. *You're not going to take away our shoeboxes that we love soooooo much . . . are you?*

"You're a monster," I told Laurence.

Similar stays of execution were also granted to a few stray plastic bottle caps ("Fanny loves 'hunting' them, and she never gets to hunt anything real," I implored); a nest of ink-less pens that Clayton, unbeknownst to us, had been hoarding beneath the couch (I tried to get rid of them, really I did—but Clayton had hippity-hopped after me, as I clutched his treasure trove of useless pens, with such a persistent and plaintive chorus of *Meeeeeeeee!* that I'd been forced to relent); some old rolls of wrapping paper that didn't have enough paper left on them to wrap another gift, but that nonetheless delighted the cats with the crinkling sound they made when they were knocked onto their sides and batted across a tile floor; and a couple of ancient bed pillows that were well past any ability to provide comfort to human heads, but that the cats thought were absolutely *purr*-fect spots for a long siesta, once Laurence and I were up and out of bed for the day.

In the end, we got rid of two huge trash bags' worth of moth-chewed clothing and a far more modestly sized bag of broken hangers, old papers, and the like, culled from our cleaning efforts throughout the rest of the house. "It's not as much as I thought it would be," I admitted to Laurence, who sighed and agreed, "Yeah . . . it never is."

Our first battle against the moths was over. The war, however, had only begun.

2. Fanny Frenzy

It's hard to imagine two creatures whose lives more closely resemble an airtight cocoon of security and love than my cats. They came to us as a "bonded pair" of littermates and best friends, and—except for the two weeks Clayton spent recovering from the surgery to remove his bad half-leg—the two of them have never been separated since the day they were born. They live with a pair of humans who dote on them to a fairly ludicrous degree and who work from home, ensuring that Clayton and Fanny have a near-constant stream of attention and affection pretty much on tap. Our leafy street in Jersey City is generally quiet and serene, and the rhythms of Clayton's and Fanny's days—varied mostly by whether and how many squirrels and birds perch on our windowsills to tempt our little would-be predators—have the sort of comforting and predictable sameness that would be the envy of most other cats.

And life, for the most part, has always been good to Clayton and Fanny. Unlike so many rescue cats, they never spent a single day of their existence confined to a cage in a shelter. They were found at two weeks of age in the backyard of a kindly cat rescuer who turned them over immediately to a foster network he volunteered with, called Furrever Friends, which placed the two kittens in the home of an experienced kitten foster mom. From what I could tell in our conversations prior to my adopting them, she lavished on Clayton and Fanny (then named Peeta and Katniss—possibly the only genuine hardship they've ever had to endure) nearly as much slavish adoration as Laurence and I do now.

It's true that I can't account for anything that may have happened to them during the first two weeks of their lives. But, then, I doubt that Clayton and Fanny would have much information to offer about those two weeks, either.

So it irks me, probably more than it should, when the two of them get more skittish than a given situation seems to call for. I expect—and accept—a certain amount of hissing from Clayton when I run the vacuum cleaner. But I'll admit that I get a wee bit impatient when I hear that same wild flurry of hissing upon snapping open a plastic garbage bag ("When," I'll ask Clayton, "have I ever allowed *a single bad thing* to happen in this house?"). Or when Fanny, the quintessential "daddy's girl," bolts in terror at the sound of Laurence's footsteps—his tread undeniably heavier than my own—coming up the stairs. Usually, once she's gotten a few feet away, she'll boomerang back around to greet Laurence properly, as if having realized mid-flight, *Oh, wait—that's not the Apocalypse. It's just Laurence walking upstairs!* But after six years of hearing that exact same footfall, you'd think she'd have learned to recognize it instantly by now.

Then there was the time when Fanny got a tiny price sticker—picked up heaven knows where—stuck to one of her front paws. I found her in the hallway trying furiously, and unsuccessfully, to shake it loose. Intending only to help—and not thinking much of it—I picked her up with one hand, pulled off the sticker (it came off very easily, I should note, and didn't take a single strand of fur with it), and placed her back on the floor. The whole thing took about two seconds. Nevertheless—I kid you not—Fanny hid under the bed or ran to hide in a closet whenever she saw me coming for the next five hours. *Five hours!* The same cat who spends half her day napping sweetly in my lap while I write—a cat whom I've never once touched with anything other than gentleness and love—was now fleeing from me in abject panic because I'd pulled a tinysticker off her front paw. The nerve of it! The drama! "Fanny!" I pleaded, watching her scuttle out of my path, eyes wide with fear, as if I were Carrie at the prom. *"What is your problem? Nothing bad has EVER happened to you!"*

So I knew we were really in for it the Saturday afternoon that Fanny got her exceptionally long, snaky tail caught in one of our moth traps.

If Phase One in our war on the moths had been a general carpet-bombing of drawers and closets with moth spray, then Phase Two was all about hand-to-hand combat. Once our arsenal of mothballs and cedar hangers, and a generous application of cedar spray, had made life in closets and drawers thoroughly untenable for the invaders, they began showing themselves out in the open, in plain sight. One of them, in a frenzied flight away from a plume of cedar spray, flew right up Laurence's nose. "I think it came out my ear!" Laurence sputtered, pressing his finger against his nose to hold one nostril closed as he exhaled furiously through the other—until, finally, he saw the welcome sight of the moth exiting (considerably worse for wear) the same way it had entered.

For a good few days, it seemed as if the air in our house was thick with minute gray wings. We went on something of a rampage, whacking them with rolled-up newspapers and T-shirts—whatever was close by, basically, that could be used to crush an errant moth against a wall or the floor without damaging either. The cats were alarmed at first by the constant hiss of spray and *thwack!* of newspapers that filled our home—although they, too, were eager to get in on the action. Fanny and Clayton sometimes made their kills individually and sometimes worked as a team, with Fanny leaping high to force a moth into a downward trajectory while Clayton waited on the ground beneath her to scoop up the befuddled insect in his jaws.

In addition to the mothballs and insecticides we'd already acquired, we purchased—on the advice of several online posters who'd also dealt with moths—a slew of moth traps, which were triangular cardboard tents with sticky interiors that operated on the same premise as Roach Motels: They enticed the moths inside with a moth-attracting scent (undetectable to the human nose) and then held them fast.

We placed the moth traps atop our tallest bookcases and highest shelves—higher, we thought, than even Fanny was able to go. Clearly, however, we had underestimated the zealousness of Fanny, our little huntress, in her pursuit of airborne quarry.

Laurence and I were downstairs on the living room couch watching a movie when we first realized something was wrong. Ever the film buff, Laurence had curated a collection of giant-bug movies from the '50s for us to watch during this, our time of insect affliction. With a new appreciation, we rediscovered (or, in my case, discovered for the first time) such noteworthy entries in the subgenre as *The Deadly Mantis, Earth vs. the Spider, Tarantula!, The Wasp Woman,* and, of course, the classic *Them!,* which was about a swarm of giant, irradiated ants that sprang up in the New Mexico desert, near the nuclear test sites.

Clayton was sound asleep on my lap, so when we first heard the rapid-fire thudding of feline paws on the floor above our heads, we assumed it was, as we call it in our house, a "Fanny Frenzy"—which is when Fanny goes to town on Rosie the Rat (her favorite plaything), swatting and tossing the toy from one bedroom to the other in a burst of hyperactivity. But then we heard the clatter and thump of unknown objects flying from their perches, and the crash of a bedside lamp hitting the floor. Those noises weren't at all typical of a Fanny Frenzy. Swiftly dislodging a thoroughly unhappy Clayton, I leapt from the couch and ran upstairs to see what was going on.

The sight that greeted me as I entered our bedroom looked like a crime scene. The pillows on the bed and the pictures on the walls were all askew. Everything that had once been on top of a piece of furniture now lay in a heap below it—books had been swept from the bookcase and were lying open and bent upside down with their pages wadded up; pens and earrings had been tossed from the top of the dresser onto the floor; the lamp, clock radio, and tissue box that customarily resided on the night table were lying at odd angles on the ground. In the midst of all this chaos, Fanny was crouched on the floor. Her pupils were so dilated with fright that her golden eyes appeared black.

Glued firmly to the end of her long, long tail was one of our tented moth traps. Unable to detach it, she'd obviously tried to outrun it instead—alas, to no avail.

"It's okay, Fanny." I deliberately made my voice low-pitched and calm as I walked slowly toward her, not wanting to alarm her further. "It's okay, baby girl. Let mommy help you."

Laurence came up the stairs behind me just in time to see Fanny turn her all-pupil eyes briefly in my direction (*Don't come any closer! I REMEMBER THE STICKER!*) before darting under the bed, the triangular moth trap still stuck to her tail skipping merrily across the floor behind her. In vain, Laurence and I knelt on opposite sides of the king-size bed and then lay down on our sides, trying to get to Fanny so we could pull her out. But neither of us had arms long enough to reach the spot in the middle where she'd curled herself into the tightest ball she could manage. The only way reaching her might have been possible would have been if Laurence lifted the bed, and it seemed unwise to risk adding the complications of a back injury to the problem we already had.

So, for the moment at least, Fanny had us at a stalemate. "She'll have to come out eventually," I finally said with a sigh. Bending down, I picked up the lamp and clock radio and restored them to their appointed spots on the night table. "And she'll probably be calmer when she does."

Fanny had bolted under the bed at around one o'clock in the afternoon, and it was nearly midnight before she finally reemerged. She'd missed both her lunch and dinner—although I'd done my best to tempt her out of hiding, carrying the cans up two flights from the kitchen to the bedroom, just so I could open them next to the bed. In my experience, the sound of a can opening and the rattling of a treats bag are the two sounds likeliest to summon even the scaredy-est cat. Accordingly, I'd also gone up periodically to shake the bag of Greenies in the hallway just outside the bedroom. But Fanny had remained unmoved by either of these lures.

Some calls of nature, however, are harder to resist than others, and I think Fanny was heading for the litter box, some eleven hours later, when she finally crept down the stairs. But the sound of the moth trap dragging behind her, thumping against each step as she descended, sent her into another, quite literal, tailspin.

Fortunately for us, though, this time Fanny didn't head up and back toward the bed. Instead, she flew down the remaining stairs and began running in desperate circles around the living room. Up and over the couch, across the coffee table, onto the mantelpiece, then back down to the floor—the triangular trap on her tale a whirling mace that sent throw pillows, coasters, coffee-table books, and framed photographs into brief, dizzying flights before they crashed to the ground. Laurence and I threw up our hands to protect our faces from any flying shards of glass from the picture frames, only lowering them once Fanny was safely earthbound again among the wreckage as her spinning continued.

Clayton, clearly laboring under the misapprehension that Fanny had invented some fascinating new game (*We're running in pointless circles! Wheeeeeeeee!*) hippity-hopped after her, working desperately hard to keep up and make sure he didn't miss out on any of the "fun." I don't know if Fanny thought that Clayton was chasing her, or if his presence simply egged her on, but the harder he pursued, the faster she ran. The moth trap still attached to Fanny's tail bounced gaily between them, like a child's pull-toy.

I knew that Fanny's inevitable next move—once the futility of running in circles had fully revealed itself to her—would be to try to get back upstairs and under the bed. Accordingly, I stationed myself in front of the staircase and hunkered down like the catcher in a baseball game. Soon enough, Fanny came winging toward me. Upon seeing me waiting for her, she tried to make a last-minute swerve beyond the reach of my arms. But this time I was quicker than she was and—at last!—I scooped her up in my arms.

Shooing Clayton away with one foot, I cradled Fanny against my chest for a moment, both hands supporting her from beneath as I pressed my cheek against the top of her head and tried to slow the anxious pounding of her heart with the calmer rhythm of my own. "I've got you, Fanny," I murmured. "I've got you, little girl. It's all going to be okay."

Gesturing Laurence toward the middle of the living-room rug, I carried Fanny over and sank slowly into a cross-legged position. Holding Fanny out at both arms' length for a moment—the moth trap now dangling limply from her tail like a flag that's lost its wind—I turned Fanny around and pressed her against my side, so that my hands were still supporting her beneath her chest and hindquarters, her head was wedged firmly beneath my elbow, and her backside with the sagging moth trap was facing toward Laurence, who was now seated across from me.

"I'm going to kind of squish her against my side, so that she feels a little safer and doesn't see what's coming," I told Laurence. "And *you* are going to rip that wretched moth trap right off her tail."

Laurence, his eyes passing over Fanny as she continued to squirm, looked dubious. "I don't want to hurt her."

"It'll be fine," I assured him. "Ready?" I pressed Fanny a bit more tightly against my side.

Laurence grasped the end of Fanny's tail and, with agonizing slowness, began to peel it from the inside of the moth trap, one strand of fur at a time. Fanny struggled in earnest now, one of her hind claws raking through my shirt and into my skin. Although we kept her claws fairly well trimmed, she dug in hard, and I knew it would leave a nasty scratch.

Gritting my teeth against both the pain and Fanny's tussling, I said to Laurence, "You have to rip it off in one clean shot, like tearing off a Band-Aid."

"But I don't want to hurt her," he repeated.

"*She's* hurting *me*," I told him. "Just get it off already."

Laurence's hold on Fanny's tail tightened, as did his grip on the moth trap in his other hand. He hesitated for a second and then, with one decisive tear, tail and moth trap were finally separated. I loosened my own grip on Fanny just a little, but that was all she needed to wriggle free. Racing back upstairs, I could hear the sound of her claws skidding across the floor above us as she once again retreated under the bed. I knew we wouldn't see her again for the rest of the night.

When I examined the moth trap, I found a fuzzy black strip that Fanny's tail had left behind but, fortunately, no skin and no blood. I, however, hadn't fared as well. A few dots of blood from the scratch Fanny had given me seeped through my nightshirt. Laurence noted it, too.

"I'll go get the alcohol," he said, standing up and helping me to my feet.

"Rubbing or drinking?" I asked, hoping for the latter. And Laurence laughed, replying, "Why not both?"

By breakfast-time the following morning, Fanny and I were friends again. A good night's sleep and the welcome aroma of food after her unplanned fast the day before (Clayton, it would appear, had eaten Fanny's food as well as his own when she'd failed to show up for her meals) had done most of the work of restoring the balance between us. After her post-breakfast siesta, Fanny returned to stalking moths through the house. Laurence and I were pleased to note that their numbers were in a definite decline. And the retreat continued even after we disposed of the rest of the moth traps—which, we were forced to admit, hadn't been nearly as effective a moth deterrent as Fanny was, anyway.

People with black cats are apt to refer to them as "house panthers." It's an epithet I'd certainly never apply to my roly-poly Clayton, crazy as I am about him. But in Fanny's case, the comparison between her and her "big cat" cousins seemed apt: the precise symmetry of her lean muscles beneath her glossy black fur; the flawless grace and balance when she leapt from floor to bookcase; the hypersensitivity of the ears, eyes, and whiskers that didn't miss a single thing that moved, crept, or flew in the terrain around her.

I realized, watching Fanny prowl through the house with as much unthinking confidence in her own prowess as any panther ever had, that the constant stream of sensory input and physical awareness—which made her such a ruthlessly efficient hunter—were also the root cause of the overload that occasionally made her spook a little too easily.

You couldn't have separated the one from the other, couldn't have changed the balance without throwing the entire mechanism off its axis. Without question, Fanny could be a pain in the neck sometimes. But she was *our* pain in the neck, which was precisely why we loved her as much as we did.

And she was still—as we recognized that laundry and pesticides would take us only so far—one of the best weapons we had in our ongoing assault against the moths.

3. Scene from a Lost Harold Pinter Play

ACT ONE – SCENE ONE

INT. GWEN AND LAURENCE'S THREE-STORY BROWNSTONE IN JERSEY CITY – A SUNNY WEDNESDAY AFTERNOON

LIGHTS UP ON DOWNSTAGE LEFT: GWEN sitting at a sleek black desk in front of her laptop computer. With one hand on the keyboard, another tapping on the desk, and her eyebrows scrunched as she gazes at the laptop's screen, she's obviously deep in thought. CLAYTON, a three-legged black cat, is splayed out on her lap.

LIGHTS UP ON ELEVATED PLATFORM, DOWNSTAGE RIGHT: LAURENCE has just sat down at an old wooden desk in front of a large desktop computer. As he arranges himself on the chair, FANNY, another black cat, eagerly leaps onto his lap and daintily makes herself comfortable. LAURENCE shifts to accommodate her as he turns his head toward the offstage door and shouts to GWEN, who is one floor beneath him.

> LAURENCE: Hey! One of the cats threw up in the kitchen!
> GWEN: Okay.
> LAURENCE: Okay.
> GWEN: And . . . ?
> LAURENCE: You should clean it before it sinks into the tile and makes a permanent stain.
> GWEN: Can't you clean it? With all the moth *mishegas* I'm behind on my deadline.
> LAURENCE: I thought you'd want to look at it first.
> GWEN: Why would I want to look at it first?
> LAURENCE: I don't know . . . I thought you might want to check viscosity and breakdown.
> GWEN: What does "viscosity and breakdown" even mean?
> LAURENCE: It's from that old motor oil commercial—remember those commercials?
> GWEN [muttering]: You and your old commercials.
> LAURENCE: What'd you say?
> GWEN: I have to turn in this story to my editor tomorrow. Are you going to clean it or not?
> LAURENCE: I really think you should examine it first.
> GWEN: They probably just ate too many moths or threw up a hairball or something.
> LAURENCE: It doesn't look like moths or a hairball.
> GWEN: How would *you* know what a hairball looks like? You never clean up their hairballs.

LAURENCE: Because I always think you'll want to look at it first.

GWEN: *Why* do you keep saying that? *What* do you think is so compelling about a puddle of cat vomit that I have to drop everything and race over like it was a flash sale at Barneys?

LAURENCE: What if one of them is sick?

GWEN: Cats throw up sometimes. It's what they *do*. I'm sure it's fine.

LAURENCE: But you don't *know* that it's fine—you don't even know who threw up.

GWEN: What am I, a cat CSI unit? How am I supposed to know which cat threw up? Was one of them standing near it?

LAURENCE: They were both gone by the time I found it.

GWEN: Found it and left it for me, you mean.

LAURENCE: I can never clean it as well as you can.

GWEN: Oh, come *on*!

LAURENCE: It's true! I'm not as good as getting it all up as you are.

GWEN: Well, as my mother used to say, *practice makes perfect.*

LAURENCE: Did she?

GWEN: She *also* used to say, *God gave you two arms and two legs.* Didn't your mother ever say anything like that?

LAURENCE: Don't bring my mother into this.

GWEN: I'm sure she'd agree that you're a grown man who's perfectly capable of cleaning up cat vomit all by himself.

LAURENCE: But I'm on the third floor. You're so much closer.

GWEN: Wait... you're *up*stairs? I thought you were still downstairs. How'd you get all the way *up*stairs?

LAURENCE: I walked on the two legs God gave me.

GWEN: Sarcasm's definitely your best play right now.

LAURENCE: Why are you asking a question you already know the answer to?

GWEN: So... you saw the throw-up on the first floor, decided to leave it for me, walked all the way past me on the second floor without saying a word, and now you're on the third floor?

LAURENCE: I can make you a sketch of my route, if you'd like.

GWEN: Very cute.
LAURENCE: Well, I'm obviously too far away to do anything about it now.
GWEN: Only because you walked up two whole floors before you said anything!
LAURENCE: What's done is done. Besides, I thought you'd want to look at first.
GWEN: Stop saying that!
LAURENCE: It's true!
GWEN: Like I don't know that this whole *you should look at it first* routine is just so you can stick *me* with a gross job.
LAURENCE: My intentions were pure.
GWEN: *Pure?!*
LAURENCE: Not to mention that Fanny's already so comfortable on my lap. It would be cruel to disturb her.
GWEN: Don't use Fanny against me! And anyway, Clayton's on *my* lap. So we're even.
LAURENCE: But I'm up on the third floor. What am I supposed to do about cat throw-up that's all the way downstairs?
GWEN: It's too bad we had those one-way-only stairs installed. How will you *possibly* get "all the way downstairs" ever again?
LAURENCE: Now who's being sarcastic?
GWEN [mimicking him]: *Now who's being sarcastic?*
LAURENCE: I heard that!
GWEN: Isn't it enough that I just did, like, fifteen loads of laundry to get rid of the moths? Can't you do this *one* thing when you know I'm on a tight deadline?
LAURENCE: Fine! I'll go down and clean the cat vomit. Go back to your writing.
GWEN: FORGET IT! I'VE ALREADY LOST MY TRAIN OF THOUGHT!
LAURENCE: This is going to end up in your new book, isn't it?
GWEN: Don't be ridiculous . . .
Scene.

4. Ping!

> *Ahoy! Bless your eyes, here's old Bill Barley. Here's old Bill Barley, bless your eyes. Here's old Bill Barley on the flat of his back, by the Lord. Lying on the flat of his back like a drifting old dead flounder, here's your old Bill Barley, bless your eyes. Ahoy! Bless you.*
> —Charles Dickens, *Great Expectations*

I always say that when I turned forty, it was like a warranty expired. There wasn't any single catastrophic failure, but all kinds of little things started going wrong in unpredictable ways. The gradual breaking down of my previously resilient body began, in point of fact, on the night of my fortieth birthday itself. Laurence and I were celebrating in Paris and had gone out for an extravagant dinner at an over-the-top restaurant (Napoleon had courted Josephine there, our guidebooks breathlessly informed us), and the six-course meal left me—despite having always prided myself on my billy-goat stomach—wide awake and tossing for the better part of the night with the kind of intense heartburn I'd never even suspected was possible.

As the months went by, new and unmistakable signs of aging cropped up. I'd find dark hairs sprouting on my chin, whereas the hair in other, more private, regions began to fall out. Suddenly I had knees that could forecast the weather: I'd feel a certain twinge in the right one and be able to inform Laurence, with near-perfect accuracy, "It's going to rain tomorrow." Getting around New York and environs was definitely more of a challenge than it had been in younger, sprightlier days. Upon reaching the top of the endless flights of stairs at the Christopher Street PATH station in the West Village, for example, I'd find myself too winded to speak for a good minute or two.

This catalog of minor grievances could go on, but you get the point. Still, nothing truly *awful* had gone wrong until one afternoon, about a month into our moth infestation, when I was in hot pursuit of a particularly large and resilient moth that Fanny had flushed out in the living room. I had a rolled-up newspaper in one hand, and had just bent over to swat the bugger as it made a sudden dive toward the floor, when I felt a *ping!* in my lower back. And then, everything stopped.

More specifically, my legs stopped. Working, that is. The last thing I remember thinking, as I fell to my knees and cried out for Laurence, was that aging is the absolute worst thing in the world.

Well... except for the alternative.

A visit to our neighborhood chiropractor revealed no injuries of a serious nature—no herniated or slipped disk, or anything requiring drastic intervention. "Just a good old-fashioned pulled muscle," was the chiropractor's diagnosis. After cracking my spine a few times, he advised, "Spend as much time as possible lying flat on a firm surface. A firm mattress would be ideal. Everything should settle back into place within a day or two."

At the risk of making my cats sound heartless, it must be said that Clayton and Fanny are always positively elated when I'm sick enough to require a full day in bed. It's usually a cold or flu that takes me down, and the cats take great pleasure in requisitioning my heating pad (to lie on) and my box of tissues (to tear to shreds). The aspirin bottle I'll keep on the bedside night table for easy access makes a charming rattle when peremptorily swatted *off* the table to roll around on the floor—and, no doubt, my cats must ask themselves whether it wouldn't be more sensible on their humans' part to simply keep this enthralling cat toy easily accessible on the night table all the time.

But the very best part of my being sick, from the cats' point of view, is that they get to join me in bed for a full day, or—if I'm *really* sick and the cats are *really* lucky—maybe even two full days. Clayton and Fanny are longtime practitioners of snooze-all-day-ism, and they seem to regard my sick days as a possible—and promising—first step toward a permanent embrace of their lifestyle. They'll pile into bed with me, and frequently *on* me, like senior members of a cult keeping close tabs on a new initiate, making sure she doesn't begin to have second thoughts or stray from the path. If they sense that I'm about to get out of bed, one or the other of them will climb onto my chest and bring a whiskered black face as close as possible to my own. *You can't quit now,* they always seem to be saying. *You're doing so great!* And if I'm sick enough to run a fever, so much the better. Burrowing under the blankets with me, they add the not-insignificant warmth of their own furry bodies to my heightened body heat, until the space beneath the covers feels like a sauna—one that vibrates with the strength of my cats' purring contentment.

The day that my back went out, however, wasn't quite like my usual sick days. For one thing, I had no interest in lying under the covers and had Laurence shove them entirely to one side of the bed—along with the piles of clothing we were still cycling in and out of the laundry in an effort to rid ourselves of moths once and for all. Even worse, I never once turned onto my side for a delightful session of cuddling one or the other of my cats in a spoon position. I just lay there sprawled out, flat on my back, in a kind of Vitruvian Man pose. I lay so flat that I couldn't even see the TV screen across the room, or much of anything other than the ceiling. The number of moths we'd spot fluttering around the house had abated almost entirely but, from time to time over the course of that day, I'd spy one or two hovering above me. Fanny spotted them, too, and leapt onto my belly in order to use my motionless body as a springboard heavenward in her pursuit, each time prompting a loud "Oof!" from me.

Convenient a launching pad as my inert body made, it wasn't exactly Clayton's or Fanny's notion of the ideal day spent in bed with Mom. Nevertheless, there was plenty to be happy about on any day that saw me spending so much time with them. And the heating pad had been duly taken down from its closet shelf and was turned over to Clayton or Fanny every twenty minutes or so, whenever I felt I'd used it long enough for the time being. That, at least, was something.

The only real moment of consternation on that first day came in the evening, when Laurence helped me into a hot bath that I hoped would help soothe my knotted back muscles into something resembling their previous shape. Proper baths—as opposed to showers—are a rare event in our house, and Clayton and Fanny peeked anxiously over the side of the tub, occasionally daring to rise up on hind legs (or hind leg, in Clayton's case) and dip a tentative front paw into the water before quickly withdrawing it. Their little brows furrowed in anxiety and confusion. *Whatcha doin' in all that water, Mom? IT'S WATER!!!*

Eventually, however—having clearly concluded with a mental shrug that humans were just *weird* sometimes, and there was no explaining them—they sprawled out in front of the tub like two ebony-carved centurions. Perhaps they'd decided that, with my having taken this foolishness into my head, *someone* had to make sure I didn't drown. In any case, their refusal to leave the tub area so long as I was still in there made Laurence's job getting me *out* of the tub, a half hour later, needlessly complicated. ("Just step around them," Laurence kept saying patiently. While I—trying vainly to move sideways a leg that refused to go in any direction other than backward or forward—replied through gritted teeth, "I can't step *around* anything!") The cats seemed relieved as, with Laurence's help, I finally hobbled back to the bedroom and the three of us settled into bed.

They weren't nearly so sanguine, however, by the following morning. Like all cats, Fanny and Clayton are wedded to the routines that make up their typical day. One of the most important items on our daily agenda is when I get out of bed at five a.m. precisely and head down from the third-floor bedroom to the first-floor kitchen to give them their breakfast—tossing Clayton's toy mouse for a few preliminary rounds of fetch along the way.

Even when I'm down with a cold or flu, I still manage to sneeze and cough my way downstairs to feed the cats on time. So nothing in their previous experience had prepared them for this first morning after my back injury. The pain in my lower back did feel distinctly lessened when I initially woke up—although possibly that was the lingering effect of the Vicodin (left over from some dental surgery Laurence had had a few months earlier), which I'd taken before going to sleep.

Nevertheless, I couldn't sit up. I had to sort of rock from side to side until, eventually, I rolled out of bed and onto the floor in a semi-crouching position, at which point I stood up as straight as I was able and limped to the bathroom at the end of the hall. After that, staggering back to bed was all that I could manage. Walking down two flights of stairs to feed the cats—and then two flights back up again—was as unattainable a goal as climbing Everest.

The cats appeared flabbergasted as I got back into bed without having fed them. Laurence was sleeping in the guest bed in his office next door—to allow me the full and undisturbed span of our bed—and I'd advised him the night before to keep his door closed, anticipating that, when the cats found me unresponsive, they would be disinclined to wait for him to wake up on his own. There was a solid five minutes of caterwauling in the hallway as the cats did their best to rouse at least one of us—but Laurence, a sound sleeper, kept dozing undisturbed. Thanks to his closed door, they were unable to deploy any of their more aggressive tactics, like stomping onto his chest and meowing loudly into his ear.

They could, however, still use both maneuvers on me. "Laurence will be up soon, you guys," I assured them over the loud and increasingly desperate cries that were beginning to make my eardrums hurt (although I knew that "soon," given that Laurence kept a much more normal schedule than I did, wouldn't be for at least two more hours). "You'll get your breakfast—I *promise* you will."

Vexed and baffled by this unprecedented state of affairs, they were obviously working hard to figure out a way of getting me onto my feet, down the stairs, and pointed in the direction of the pantry where their food was kept. Clayton seemed to be of the opinion that if *he* kept doing the things that he normally does in the morning, then inevitably *I* would also fall back into my normal routine. Accordingly, he kept bringing over the rattling toy mouse he likes to play fetch with, hauling himself up onto the bed so he could rattle it a few times in his mouth and then drop it into my hand. I would toss it half-heartedly as far across the room as I could without moving any more of my body than my arm. Clayton was patient with me at first as he dutifully retrieved the mouse, climbed back onto the bed, and dropped it into my hand once again. *No, see, you're doing it wrong. You're supposed to* get up *and throw it for me—and then you're supposed to keep walking.* After four or five repetitions, however, he was stumped. He looked over to Fanny for guidance. *Got any ideas?*

Fanny is unquestionably the smarter of the two. She had evidently reasoned out that I couldn't solve *their* problems until my own mysterious problem—whatever it was—had also been solved. She leapt nimbly from the bed, and I heard her descending the stairs. She returned a few moments later and, with the "hunting" cry that generally meant she was about to leave Laurence or me a "gift" (usually Rosie the Rat, which she thoughtfully places on our pillows every night before bedtime), returned to my side and gently deposited a white plastic spoon on my stomach. She watched me expectantly for a few seconds, seemingly disappointed that her gift had produced no immediate effect beyond my saying, "Thank you, Fanny," and handing the spoon back to her. Undeterred, however, she departed again and returned with another white plastic spoon—and then, about three minutes later, with yet another.

I'm still not sure what these plastic spoons symbolized to Fanny (or even where this stash of hers was being kept, given the thorough moth-related housecleaning we were still in the process of undertaking). Perhaps, I reasoned, trying to follow the logic, she knew that humans use spoons for eating and thought that if I ate something, I might be able to get up? Whatever effect she'd hoped the spoons might produce, when it failed to occur she must have decided that a more drastic intervention was called for.

It was perhaps a half hour later, and I'd just drifted back into sleep, when I was roused once again by the sound of Fanny ascending the stairs with her hunting cry. I felt her land beside me on the bed, and she once again placed something on my belly. I blearily half-opened my eyes and raised my head as far as I could without engaging any more of my beleaguered spine than the very top portion of my neck. It was hard to make out what it was at first, although . . . was I imagining it? Was whatever it was *moving?* The room was still dark in the pre-dawn hours, so I switched on the bedside lamp.

It took me a second to realize what it was—primarily because my brain, for a moment, flat-out refused to confirm the report my eyes were sending. What Fanny had so lovingly deposited on my stomach was an enormous palmetto bug—otherwise known in the Northeast as a "water bug," or simply a "huge ugly cockroach"—on its back *AND STILL ALIVE* as all six of its legs waved feebly in the air.

Now, I was born and raised in South Florida. I've seen plenty of giant cockroaches in my day. I've seen—and dispatched without flinching—cockroaches so big you could've saddled and ridden them in the Kentucky Derby. I had even, once or twice, awakened with a kind of prickly sensation on my arm and realized it was just such a cockroach crawling across me.

And, as would normally be the case in finding an enormous cockroach on my person, my instinctive first response—which, without thinking, I immediately undertook—was to attempt to bolt upright into a sitting position so as to dislodge the thing and *get it off me*.

Except that I *couldn't* bolt upright. I couldn't sit upright at all. The instant and painful wrench I felt in my lower back as I tried to rise quickly—an effort that would end up costing me another two days in bed—was a forceful reminder of just how futile this attempt was. "*Son of a—!*" I swore loudly, as I fell back into a supine position.

So there I was, flailing about helplessly on my back, while the giant cockroach on my belly was *also* flailing about helplessly on *its* back, the two of us acting out a scene from some cat-and-cockroach remake of *Misery*, in which Fanny was playing the Kathy Bates role and either the cockroach or I—or both of us—were James Caan.

Ultimately, the palmetto bug was more successful than I was. It soon righted itself and began a rapid scurry up my body in the general direction of my neck. I tried to brush it off with the back of my hand but, with a brief flutter of wings, it scuttled right over the top of my hand, down my palm, and—clearly as startled and disoriented as I was—continued its trajectory up my torso with an increased dash of frenzied speed.

I had a friend in Miami who'd once awakened in the middle of the night to find that a palmetto bug had crawled into his ear, and both his own and the cockroach's combined efforts had been unable to get it back out. He'd wound up in the emergency room where the doctors irrigated his ear canal—effectively drowning the palmetto bug while my friend was forced to listen to its excruciating death throes *inside his own head*—before they were finally able to extract its corpse from his ear, chunk by chunk, with a small pair of forceps.

This palmetto bug—the one that *I* was dealing with in the here and now—was closing the distance between itself and my chin at an alarmingly swift pace.

"*Laurence!*" I shrieked. "*LAAAAUUUUUUREEEEEEN-NNCE!!!*"

Fanny and Clayton—who'd been sitting next to me with an eager air this whole time—darted off and under the bed so quickly, they practically left spinning dust clouds behind them. From the guest room, I heard the sound of feet hitting the hardwood floor and then a rapid thud of footsteps. In a flash Laurence was standing in the bedroom doorway, clad only in his boxer briefs and brandishing the baseball bat he always kept next to him while he slept (a holdover from having first moved to New York in the '80s, at the height of the crack epidemic).

So poised and ready did Laurence look to club somebody bloody with that baseball bat that I had a wild, momentary fear he might use it on the cockroach while it was still on top of me.

"Get it off me," I whimpered, gesturing to the bug on my chest. "*Get it off me!*"

Dropping the bat with a clatter and grabbing a handful of tissues from the box on our night table, Laurence snatched up the hapless cockroach. He clenched his fist with a satisfying crunch and swept it from the room, the sound of the toilet flushing a moment later confirming that it had been given a burial at sea.

"How did it get all the way up here, anyway?" he asked, as he returned to the bedroom. During the warmer months, we were usually good for one or two palmetto bugs a week squeezing into the basement-level kitchen through the French doors that led out to our tiny backyard. But the only time we ever saw one up on the third floor was in pieces, after Fanny had thoroughly mauled it and left its remains for us as an offering.

"Fanny brought it up," I confirmed. "I think she thought she was 'helping.' She didn't even eat any of it before she gave it to me." The thudding of my heart had finally slowed to its normal rhythms, and I smiled at Laurence. "That was damn manly, by the way—how you raced in here ready to beat an intruder to death to protect me."

Laurence smiled back. "I probably would've tried to talk my way out of it first."

Clayton and Fanny, having determined that the coast was clear, peeked out from beneath the bed's dust ruffle, then tentatively crept over to sit in front of Laurence. They craned their necks to gaze up into his face, their yellow eyes wide and hopeful. "You know," I suggested, "as long as you're awake . . ."

Laurence looked down at the cats. "Come on, guys," he said, his tone resigned. "Let's go get breakfast."

Fanny gave Clayton a look that could only be described as triumphant. *See? I knew I could get at least one of them out of bed!*

As the three of them headed downstairs, one lone moth fluttered out of a dresser drawer to perch on the ceiling above my head—a solitary soldier in the enemy army taunting me, a fallen warrior, as I lay helplessly on my back remembering the day, one pleasant but otherwise ordinary day, just over a year ago when the whole thing had started.

5. In the Beginning . . .

It was a dreamily perfect spring afternoon. The sky outside the window of my writing nook was as pure and crystalline a blue as God had ever intended. The tiny pink roses on the climbing bush, wending its way up the wooden fence enclosing our small backyard, were in full, festive bloom. After a particularly cold and difficult winter, the entire backyard had exploded into a riot of glorious green leaf and multihued flower. I'll admit that there are still days when I think to myself that nothing will ever be better than living in Manhattan. But, on days like that one, I can't imagine any place on Earth I'd rather be than in my lovely little brownstone, here in Jersey City, with Fanny napping on the sunlit windowsill of my writing nook and Clayton dozing peacefully on the desk beside me.

A sudden commotion of sparrows split the silence outside, and I swiveled in my desk chair to see what had them so agitated. A wispy, fast-moving cloud of some kind was rising from the other side of the fence that adjoined our neighbor's yard. I couldn't tell what it was at first, but I soon detected the fluttering of small, almost imperceptible wings. It looked as if an egg sac of infant moths had burst open into the stillness of the springtime air—and the sparrows, grateful for the bounty, had stationed themselves in a cluster around the newly hatched insects, gobbling up as many as they could in their small beaks as the moths tried to beat their way skyward.

The sound of sparrows tittering in the backyard had wakened Fanny and Clayton from their slumber, and they took up side-by-side positions on the windowsill for a better look. My wall-unit air conditioner faces out onto the backyard, and soon I noticed three or four of the minuscule moths—small enough to pass through the filter—fluttering their way through the air conditioner, into the house, and around the cats' heads.

It was the birds my cats wanted, not the bugs. But the cats were already up, their appetite for hunting whetted, and the baby moths were better than nothing. Rising up on her hind legs, Fanny tried to grab at them with her front paws, while Clayton made a few half-hearted hops, attempting to catch one or two in his mouth before they got away.

But the moths were so small—so very, very tiny—that it was nearly impossible to keep track of them among the dust motes also dancing in the sunlight that fell through the window. Almost before Clayton and Fanny had even started to try to catch the insects, before I could think of finding something to swat at them with myself, the wee creatures had flitted out of sight. And even though they hadn't tried *very* hard to nab the moths, Fanny and Clayton still looked disappointed.

"Aw, don't worry about *them*, you guys," I said, giving each cat a sympathetic scritch on the head. Fanny and Clayton looked up at me drowsily from heavy-lidded golden eyes, purring lightly at the touch of my hand. "Those silly moths weren't worth trying to eat, anyway. There'll be plenty of bigger and better things for you two to catch someday. You'll see . . ."

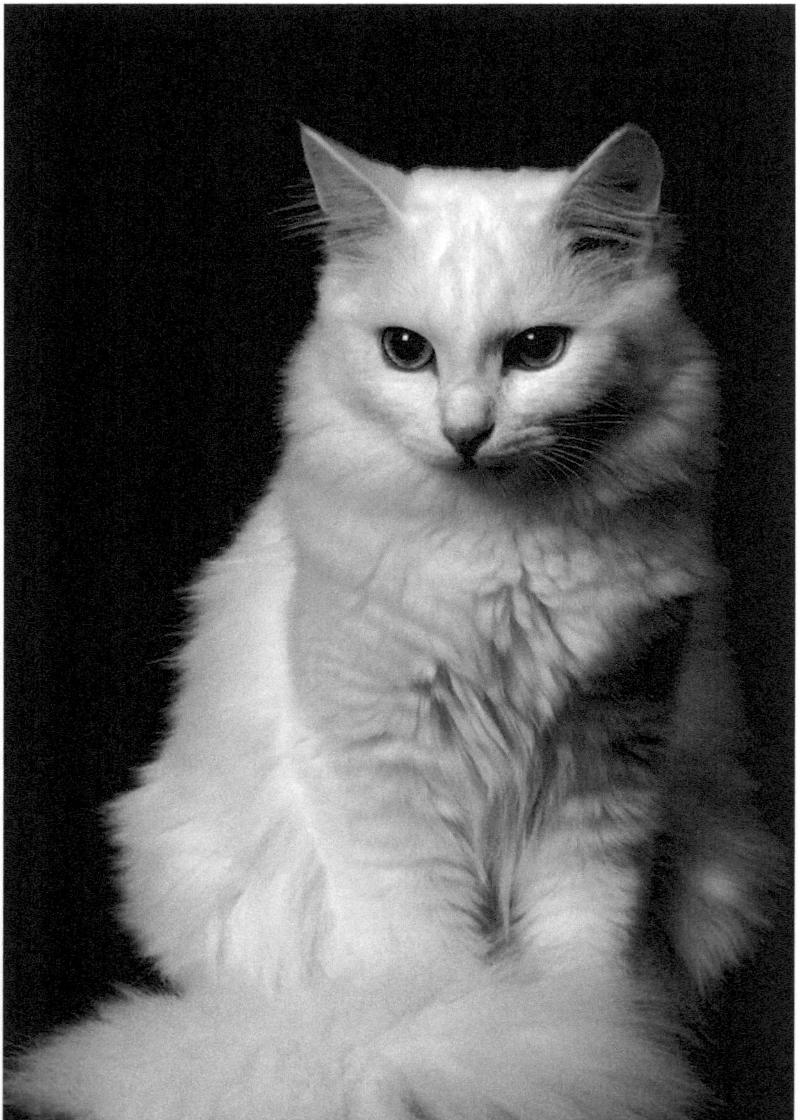

Love in a Cold Climate

IT WAS JANUARY OF 2001, and every job interview I had in New York started with the same question: "You want to move to New York—in *January*—from Miami Beach?"

Sometimes this would be followed by the interviewer rhapsodizing about how his or her secret dream was making the reverse move of the one I contemplated—from Manhattan to South Beach instead of vice versa. Sometimes reference would be made to the temperature, currently hovering in the twenties in New York City, thermometers struggling to rise beneath a thick blanket of slate-gray clouds that wouldn't let a single ray of sunshine through, yet also stubbornly refused to yield the gentle snowfall that might have cloaked the city in a hint of romance. Sometimes the interviewer would simply wave a hand to indicate a frost-covered window—which, to my benighted eyes, looked glittery and dazzling, the secret, overnight work of the snow fairies I'd read about in books as a child. But to the typical New Yorker, it meant only one thing: *It's freaking COLD out there!*

Always, however, the question would be asked in the sort of incredulous, are-you-*crazy?!* tone only a true New Yorker can muster—as if I'd announced that, after the interview, I intended to treat myself to the finest Italian meal New York City had to offer...at the Times Square Olive Garden.

South Beach, where I currently lived, was the land of bare skin and beaches—of white sands, turquoise waters, and year-round tans. My apartment building boasted an Olympic-sized swimming pool, which could be comfortably enjoyed for all but perhaps two uncharacteristically cold weeks out of the year. A mere thirty feet from that pool was Biscayne Bay, where one could go boating or jet skiing even (and especially) in the depths of January. From the balcony of my spacious one-bedroom apartment, I could look to the left and see the Bay, and to the right I could see the ocean itself, its waters closest to shore dotted with puffy white windsurfing sails and colorful floats upon which sunbathers bobbed along and, a bit farther out, the occasional cigarette boat zooming along, leaving a barely discernible wake.

Only a truly insane person, the raised eyebrows of my interviewers strongly implied, would consider trading this paradise for the purgatory of New York City in winter.

"Hell is hot all year round, too," I'd quip, "but nobody wants to live there." By this, I didn't mean to imply that my life in South Beach could be described as "hellish." Far from it. But I did feel—with all the confidence of a person who'd never had to stand a truly cold climate for more than five consecutive days in her entire life—that warm weather wasn't everything. Like a person who's always been so wealthy that she truly can't understand why people make such a fuss about *money*, of all things, I took sunshine and soft, salt-scented breezes for granted. I didn't think it was *nothing*, but it hardly made sense to arrange one's whole life around so trivial a consideration.

I wasn't a masochist, and the decision to move to New York wasn't one I'd arrived at lightly. I didn't work in tourism, hospitality, or international finance—just about the only stable industries in Miami. I worked in corporate marketing communications and, since I didn't have a background in any of the aforementioned fields, my only real job opportunities had come from the kind of fly-by-night companies that sprang up like dandelions and disappeared just as quickly from Miami's ever-shifting economic landscape. I wanted to work for a media company—print or online ("online" still being a fairly new word in the common parlance), it didn't matter to me. I wanted to work with people who created written content for a large audience, and I had a vague hope that I, myself, might someday be one of those people who created that written content.

Plus, I'd always been more partial to cityscapes than beachscapes, anyway. I loved tall buildings, small sidewalk cafes, live theater, and quirky little shops that weren't part of a national chain. In my mind's fanciful eye, I saw myself with chic coats and jackets, sweaters in my closet (a closetful of sweaters—imagine it!) that varied in thickness, so that some made more sense for the early days of fall while others were clearly best suited for the late days of winter. I imagined suede boots with high heels that would rap confidently along concrete sidewalks, adding two—or perhaps even three—inches to my height.

There's no such thing as "living" in New York—there's only surviving there, a writer friend of mine, a New York transplant to Miami, had warned me. But I pooh-poohed the notion. New York was where I wanted to be. My twenty-ninth birthday had just passed, and my thirtieth was looming on the horizon—which meant there was no better time than the present.

I ended up receiving a few job offers, one of which came with the added bonus of covering my moving expenses. The die was cast. On January 29th of 2001, just over two weeks before Valentine's Day, my three cats and I moved from our roomy South Beach one-bedroom into a small studio in Manhattan.

THE COLD WAS BEWILDERING to all of us at first—my cats as well as me. It howled around our new corner apartment way up on the thirty-first floor. You could actually hear the cold wind whipping around outside our windows at night as if demanding to be let in, which caused the four of us to shiver closer together (or as close as the ever-aloof Scarlett would allow the other cats to get to her) beneath the thick comforter I'd packed into an extra checked suitcase on our plane ride up. Vashti, out of all of us, was perhaps genetically best suited for cold weather, with her thick snowy fur and the tufts of white that sprang from beneath the pink pads of her paws, like built-in snowshoes. But even she was stunned into a certain sluggishness for the first few days, the three of them—including Homer, usually such a little bundle of activity—spending most of their time either sleeping or wandering around the confines of our new, tiny apartment in a disoriented way, territorially staking out warm spots on the floor for the hour in the mornings when sunlight (if it wasn't cloudy) fell directly through the windows.

Homer was particularly confused by the fact that we were now living in a single room, a turn of events that not only didn't jibe with anything in his previous experience, but which was, apparently, beyond even his conceptual understanding. He seemed convinced there was a door that would lead to another room, somewhere, if only he could find it, whining and pawing fretfully at the plaster whenever his nose or whiskers encountered a wall where it seemed clear to him that a door ought to be. Scarlett and Vashti, unlike Homer, could *see* that our new apartment was, indeed, as small as it felt. They could also tell that the sound of the wind outside wasn't made by an actual creature seeking entrance. But not so with Homer. Sometimes I woke in the night to hear him hiss in alarm as a particularly strong gust of wind tore loudly around the outside of our walls. *Stay out! We don't need any more cold in here!*

It didn't help that our heater—which should have been able to ward off any feeling of cold inside, even if it couldn't stop the sound of it outside—periodically made a startlingly loud buzzing sound, and then clanked and clonked four or five times, before releasing (evidently with great reluctance) a hiss of warm air into the room. *Buzzzzzzzz! Clank! Clank! CLONK! hisssssss*, went the heater, always provoking my over-protective Homer into wild frenzies of hissing and clawing at he-knew-not-what (some unidentifiable monster who, for inexplicable reasons, had moved in with us, I always imagined him thinking). One time he landed a full-clawed blow on the heater's metal grating and his paw remained stuck there, a single claw lodged in the grate and refusing to budge, and I had to come to his aid. Knowing nothing about heaters—having literally never lived with one before—it took me about a month longer than it should have to realize that this wasn't normal heater behavior, and to call the super to come up and replace it. By then it was March, and the weather was starting to turn warmer anyway. But for that first month, I ended up switching the heater off much of the time, preferring even the cold to all the racket.

It also didn't help that we were living in our New York apartment for more than two weeks before our furniture was finally delivered from Miami. I had ditched quite a few pieces (most notably a loveseat and dining set) before my move, since I wouldn't have been able to come close to fitting everything from my old place into my new one. The resulting shipment was so small, it wasn't worth the moving company's time to bring it up north until they were able to combine it with another. (Apparently, there were at least two of us half-baked enough to move from Miami to New York in the winter.) In the meantime, I had to make do with an air mattress that kept mysteriously deflating over the course of the night, causing me to wake up with aching bones atop a pancake-flat rubber swath that was the only cushion between my joints and cold, hardwood floors. I nearly blinded myself, so closely did I scrutinize every millimeter of that air mattress, looking for even the smallest tear or hole that I could patch up. I never found one, though, and so had to continue camping out on the cold floors of the "luxury" apartment I was paying far too much to live in, all things considered.

The cats fared slightly better at night than I did, able to curl up on top of me, or on some particularly thick wedge of the quilt, and find comfort that way. We all became very close those first weeks. Vashti, in particular, was fond of draping herself across my neck at night like a boa. I'd awaken from dreams of being smothered by giant marshmallows during a prison riot (dreams fueled by a particularly loud *Clank! Clank! CLONK!* from the heater) to find that Vashti's luxurious plume of a tail had fallen across my mouth and nose while we'd slept. Once, before I was fully awake, I ended up inhaling rather a sizeable wad of Vashti's tail fur through my open mouth and then spent the rest of the subsequent workday, to my eternal embarrassment, struggling with the resultant hairball that had lodged in my throat. "Are you okay?" various coworkers asked in concerned tones, as I coughed and retched my way through meetings. "Seasonal allergies," I claimed weakly, once I'd stopped wheezing long enough to squeeze out of a few words.

I'm not sure that they believed me, but anything was better than saying, *Don't mind me—I'm just coughing up a hairball!* "How do you guys *live* with this?!" I demanded of my cats when I got home that night. I'd often said that my fondest wish would be to come back in a future life as one of my own pampered cats—but if hairballs were part of the deal, I found myself thinking now, I might have to reconsider.

I spent a lot of time talking to my cats during those early days right after my move—simply because there wasn't much else to *do*. There was nothing at all in my apartment aside from the deflating air mattress, my comforter and two pillows, a couple of books, a clock radio, a telephone, a litter box and food bowls—and, of course, my cats. After nightfall—which, its being February, occurred well before I got home from work—light came from the overhead bulbs in the kitchen and bathroom, left on continuously until I went to sleep. Still, there wasn't much light in the apartment except for the spot directly under the kitchen's fluorescent, which made reading a book challenging unless I propped my back against a cabinet while sitting on the cold tile of the kitchen floor—not exactly a comfortable position to settle into for a few hours with a good novel.

The cats' eyes glowed from the shadows of our mostly dark apartment, and I often sensed that they reflected a hint of accusation. *Why did you move us to this cold, empty place? We were so happy where we were!* "Hey—it's hard for me, too!" I said aloud, more than once, which was usually about the time I realized that I needed to hear a human voice if I were to get through the rest of the long night ahead. I'd pick up the phone to call friends still back in South Beach, lounging poolside or preparing to head out to the launch party for one or the other of this year's hot new SoBe clubs, which was invariably opening in what had formerly been the site of one of last year's hot new SoBe clubs.

It was precisely what I'd frittered away too much of my twenties doing—what I'd moved to New York to get away from as I charted a new, more serious path into my impending thirties. So there was really no reason, I'd remind myself, to feel as homesick as I did during these conversations, pulling one of my cranky cats into my arms and stroking them until the build-up of static electricity in their fur—created by the cool, dry air of our new home—forced me to stop. That I even found myself missing Miami's oppressive humidity was a sign of how homesick I was. Sure, all the moisture in the air had frequently left me with a tangle of frizzy curls that looked as if it should have adorned the head of a circus clown. But at least I'd been able to pet my cats as much as I wanted without having to worry about shocking them into hostility.

I always ended up cutting these phone calls short, and the friend I was talking to would always promise, "I'll tell everyone you send your love!" before hanging up. Then I'd turn on my static-y clock radio, to relieve the dead silence of our apartment way up on the thirty-first floor, and release my equally static-y cat. He or she would run off to pass a static-electric shock to a resentful brother or sister, who'd recoil reproachfully (*Hey! What was that for?!*) at the little spark that flew between them when their noses touched.

BOTH THE COLD AND the sheer, overwhelming size of the city I now officially lived in were intimidating and conspired to keep me indoors for the first few days. But I couldn't spend all my non-work hours sitting alone in a dark apartment, and so I began taking long walks at night and on the weekend. I was trying to figure out Manhattan's byzantine subway system (legend has it that there's still no entirely accurate map of all its tunnels and stops) and, standing on platforms and waiting for trains to arrive, blasts of cold air would whip through the tunnels, blowing my hair back, whenever a train was about to make an appearance. The old leather bomber jacket my father had handed down to me before I'd left Miami was no match for the cold outside. I also lacked gloves or a good, thick scarf, and even the handful of sweaters I'd accrued over the years in Miami weren't as warm as I would have liked. *It'll be different next winter,* I'd tell myself. *Next year, I'll be able to afford everything I need.* For now, though, there wasn't much I could do beyond stamping my feet and breathing warm air onto my hands as I rubbed them together, before shoving them into the too-large pockets of my dad's old jacket, which still let in entirely too much cold air for comfort.

And yet, it was undeniably exciting to walk around this sprawling, hectic, over-stimulating urban landscape I now called home. The buildings and shop windows all lit up at night like Christmas trees, promising the warmth inside that was denied to those of us outside on the pavement. Crowded as they were, though, with masses of people scurrying frantically to and fro, the pavements of Midtown were still warmer than they were down in the Financial District, where I lived, which almost completely emptied out after five o'clock. Walking through Soho on a sunny Saturday afternoon—thronged with trendy weekend shoppers, even in the middle of February—it was almost possible to forget how cold it truly was.

I was delighted to find, as I rambled along with no particular destination, small bodegas and bookstores that actually had "shop cats" in residence. I'd never encountered shop cats in Miami, and finding an ordinary place of business that had a cat dwelling in its inner recesses felt like discovering some hidden world, accessible only to a select few who knew where to look. And I also found more small, quirky pet stores than I would have thought one city could hold. My shopping for pet supplies back home had primarily taken place in superstores like Petco and PetSmart, whereas here in New York there was an endless array of mom-and-pop options—each with its own distinct personality and brand of shop clerks, ranging from morose hipsters, whose sulky expressions clearly conveyed that they were bored out of their wits, to comfortable-looking middle-aged cat ladies who were more than happy to engage in earnest conversations about which food or toy might best suit a particular cat's health needs and personality. I felt like a true New Yorker—a tribe famed for being short of temper and long on opinions—the Sunday morning when I got into a heated argument with the proprietor of an all-vegan pet shop as to whether it was healthy, or even possible, to feed cats, obligate carnivores as everyone knows, an all-vegan diet. (It's not, and you shouldn't.) To this day, that store remains the one and only retail establishment from which I've ever been banned for life. As if, I haughtily informed the righteously indignant proprietor, I would even *think* of visiting *that* store again.

Most of my encounters were far more positive, however. I was constantly finding little things to bring home for the cats—exotic new flavors and varieties of cat treats, imaginatively decorated brands of canned food that I'd never encountered back in Miami. I bought little bags of catnip and three heated cat beds that could be plugged into the wall—so that the cats would have something warm and soft to sleep on, even if I didn't. My reward was the first genuine demonstration of feline contentment I'd seen since the move, as all three of my cats rolled around on their backs in custom-heated ecstasy, high on warmth and the 'nip I'd sprinkled judiciously all over the soft plush before plugging the cat beds in.

I even bought a new kitty condo, which all three of them could climb to the top of (and finally have something to perch on in our new place), although only Vashti and Scarlett could ascend its heights and then peer down from the tops of our tall windows on the thirty-first floor to take occasional, pointless swipes at birds flying by, or gaze down like all-powerful gods on the antlike humans scurrying about far below them.

I guilt-shopped more than I should have for the cats, filling my apartment full of cat stuff as a substitute for the actual furniture I still hadn't been able to make materialize, despite near-daily phone calls to the moving company. A stranger visiting my apartment—and seeing my deflated air mattress, shoved into one corner with my comforter and pillows like a rat's nest, and then taking in all the cat toys and cat beds and the new cat condo—would likely have concluded that I was some sort of crazy cat lady who'd "gone to the mattresses" while lamming it from mafia hitmen.

Perhaps the only disheartening thing about all the time I spent out of doors—aside from the cold itself, which was brutal and unrelenting—were the festive windows of jewelry stores and card shops and restaurants, all proclaiming the imminent arrival of Valentine's Day. I would be alone this year—utterly alone in a way I never had been before. It wasn't as if I'd left some great boyfriend behind in Miami (had there been a great boyfriend, I likely wouldn't have moved away in the first place). And it certainly wasn't as if I'd never before borne witness to excited women in my office whose desks, for that one day, were adorned with colorful bouquets and heart-shaped boxes of candy while my own desk remained bare of all such baubles. I'd never even really cared all that much about Valentine's Day, truth be told—not even when I'd had boyfriends to spend the holiday with.

But this would be the first year when I wouldn't have the option of hanging out with a group of friends—to watch a marathon of rom-coms (if we were feeling aspirational) or action movies (if we felt like going against the romantic mood of the day)—while we reassured each other that we were all fabulous and would eventually be appreciated by The Right Person, who simply hadn't materialized yet, and that everybody knew Valentine's Day was just a made-up Hallmark holiday, anyhow. I was still young enough to feel that arbitrary calendar dates amounted to milestones against which I was supposed to be measuring my progress in life—and this last Valentine's Day of my twenties didn't seem to offer much in the way of positive reflections on what I'd accomplished with my life thus far.

And I wouldn't even be able to watch those rom-coms or action movies on my own. I still had no TV, no DVD player. There was literally nothing in my apartment to watch or look at, aside from my cats.

AND WATCH MY CATS, I did. I watched them as they slept in their new beds, and as Homer—creeping along quietly and believing, as always, that "silent" and "invisible" were the same thing—attempted to annex Scarlett's bed the moment she got out of it, receiving an imperious slap of her front paw as his reward. I watched as all three of them began engaging in extraordinarily elaborate grooming rituals, attempting to combat the static electricity that made the job of ridding themselves of pesky bits of stray fur and dust far more onerous than it had been back in Miami. Their own shed fur clung to them, as did fur from the other cats. Strands of Vashti's white fur stuck to Homer's ebony coat—or vice versa—and Scarlett's gray tabby tufts, which occupied a sort of hued middle ground between them, were conspicuous on all three cats. And no matter how much I tried to clean (which wasn't too hard, since there wasn't any furniture), if there was a single speck of dust or strand of my own hair floating around, it seemed to find its way eventually to my cats' flanks and tails, held fast by a static-electric charge.

All the extra grooming forced my cats to roll onto their backs more than usual, to reach those hard-to-get spots, and of course all the extra rolling just made more static accumulate in their fur. I'd never thought much about how often or vigorously my cats groomed themselves—cats' grooming had, for some years now, simply been a part of the "background noise" of my everyday life, like the way you stop hearing the crashing of the tides when you live on a beach. But, with so little else to pay attention to—without the blare of the television or a constantly ringing phone to distract me—I noticed it now. I started noticing, or at least consciously thinking about, other things, too. Things I realized I'd known on some level all along, but had stopped paying attention to somewhere along the way.

I'd always felt that I knew the three of them well, of course. I was their "mom." Who could possibly know my cats better or more intimately than I did? I'd always thought of myself as a conscientious cat custodian, able to recite, at a moment's notice, complete personal and medical histories, food preferences, sleeping habits, and so on.

But, during our first two weeks in New York, I got to know them even better than I already had—and to wonder about things that I might have noticed before, but had never contemplated the meaning of. Scarlett, for example, always kicked her left hind leg twice when exiting the litter box. She was the most fastidious of all my cats, and hated tracking even a speck of litter outside of the box if she could help it. But, even if there weren't any obvious particles clinging to her fur when she exited, she still always did that little two-step kick before she considered her business concluded. Why?

Was it merely a habit? Some sort of obsessive-compulsive ritual that she couldn't have rid herself of, even if she'd wanted to? Had some unwelcome tagalong from the litter box once stuck to her back paw in her younger days, irritating her for hours and leaving an indelible impression that persisted even all these years later? Or perhaps, I reflected, this was new behavior since our move to New York, some response to our new environment that made some kind of logical sense to Scarlett, even if its logic wasn't at all apparent to me.

Scarlett was also the least inherently trusting of my cats—and yet, she was the only one who ever slept sprawled out on her back, four white paws in the air with her white tummy exposed to whoever might happen by. To make herself so vulnerable when she slept—the time when she was already most vulnerable to begin with—seemed incongruous with what I knew of Scarlett's personality. It was a genuine puzzle, when I paused to give it some thought, and one that I still don't have an entirely satisfactory answer to—beyond noting that Scarlett had gained, by far, the most weight of any of them over the years, and at a certain point she was probably most comfortable simply letting it all hang loose, so to speak.

Vashti liked to sleep in a loaf-of-bread posture, on her belly with her head up and her four little paws tucked beneath her. And she never drank water directly from her water bowl—or from the bathtub faucet, which she occasionally pestered me about until I turned it on for her. Instead, she'd daintily dip a paw into the water and then, when it was thoroughly soaked, lick the droplets from her paw. It was a habit that I'd been dimly aware of, but had always thought of it as her "washing her hands." I tried now to remember if I'd ever seen her actually lapping water directly from a water source, and found that I couldn't recall a single instance of it. And wasn't that an odd thing to notice for the first time about a cat I'd been living with for nearly six years?

Every morning, and despite his blindness, Homer unerringly found, with the accuracy of a heat-seeking missile, the warm patch of sunlight that fell through our windows onto the floor at eight a.m. The pure coal black of his fur glowed a warm chocolatey brown in direct sunlight, with tabby stripes of a slightly darker brown, and how was it possible that I'd never realized before, or even thought about, how heart-stoppingly beautiful that was? Whenever he slept in the sun, he liked to fling one paw over the space where his eyes would have been—another thing I'd noticed but never really considered. It wasn't as if the brightness of the light falling across his face would have woken him up. Was it an instinctive response to the heat, the way the muscles around his sockets tightened, as if he were blinking, if a blast of air hit his face?

Homer, in some ways, fared better than the rest of us—not only because the darkness of our lamp-less apartment at night couldn't possibly matter to him, but also because I'd packed his beloved stuffed worm into his carrier with him when we'd flown from Miami to New York. He, at least, had something well-loved and familiar to keep him company in this strange new place. I'd been cognizant enough of his love for that worm to think to pack it with him when we traveled, but I hadn't given it much consideration aside from, *Homer really likes that worm.* I thought now, though, what an odd thing it was that *this* bedraggled, slightly woebegone toy—of all the things I'd so lovingly set before Scarlett in the earliest days of her kitten-hood—had been the one and only store-bought toy that had stood the test of time, cherished by all three of my cats in their turn until it had finally fallen to Homer, who'd claimed it definitively as his own special property. As much as Scarlett and Vashti had enjoyed it before him, they'd never fallen asleep with it between their front paws, as Homer habitually did, one whiskered cheek resting peacefully atop it in the sunlight.

I'd toss a crumpled up piece of paper I'd filched from my new office for Scarlett and Vashti's entertainment (we had to have *something* to do to kill the time, after all), and remember what a very hard time Scarlett had given me with her resolute indifference to me, and to anything having to do with me, during our earliest days together, when she was still the first and only cat I'd ever lived with. For the past year or so, she'd come to cuddle up next to me on a fairly regular basis, and how was it possible that I'd forgotten to remember what an extraordinary turn of events that was? And Vashti's love of fetch! One night Vashti brought me a straight piece of paper that she'd nicked from the windowsill where (in lieu of a desk or a dresser or *anything at all* with drawers or shelves) I'd taken to storing work supplies, clearly intending that I should crumple and throw it for her, so she could retrieve it for me to throw again. Vashti hadn't been especially interested in fetch since she was a kitten—but, as a kitten, fetch had been a deep and abiding passion of hers. But I hadn't thought about that at all—hadn't even remembered it—in at least four years.

I noticed this, and a million other little things—the way Scarlett would always use her front right paw to spill three kibbles of dry food onto the floor, and then eat them from the ground, before dipping her head into the bowl to eat properly. The way Vashti would stand in a patch of sunlight, lift her head, and half-close her eyes for a moment, basking in the warmth, before ceding the sunny spot to Homer with remarkable good grace. The way Homer's tail would puff up slightly only at its base, whenever he vibrated it with the joy of encountering me upon our waking up first thing in the morning.

I realize that this all sounds like ridiculous minutiae—the inevitable result of a bored mind with far too little to occupy it. And, without question, it was. But I can also say with complete honesty that I likely would never have become a cat writer, some seven or eight years later, if not for this period of enforced reveries, during which I got to know my cats from scratch, all over again.

🐾 🐾

KEEP IN MIND THAT this was only a two-week period that I'm writing about. If it seems longer in my memory now, or in the retelling, it's probably because the swiftness and entirety of the change between my old life—loaded with friends, beach days, and a cheerful, cluttered apartment—and this new, decidedly emptier, one couldn't have been a greater shock. And I have to think all the way back to my go-round with chicken pox in my early twenties (yikes) to recall a more physically uncomfortable two weeks I've ever experienced. There were days when I honestly worried that

I might be developing a hunch, or encouraging some other sort of incipient spinal deformity, from sleeping on that ever-deflating mattress that offered essentially nothing in the way of cushion between my back and the floor. By the time Valentine's Day finally rolled around, I didn't need to worry about feeling sorry for myself while looking at all the bouquets and stuffed teddy bears, holding little stuffed hearts, on my female coworkers' desks. It was literally impossible for me to turn my neck in any direction, so many pinched nerves did I have. I could focus only on the computer screen and work directly in front of me on my own desk—which, I suppose, was good for my productivity, if not for my state of mind.

Every moment when the cats actually seemed happy in their new home, I counted as a triumph. Every moment when they seemed unhappy or uncomfortable, I asked myself whether I had, in fact, ruined their lives—which of course naturally made me wonder if I'd managed to ruin my own as well. Of all the things I'd thought about when contemplating this move, static electricity hadn't even been among them—and yet, the dry and hyper-charged air of our new home was probably the most disconcerting thing for all of us. I couldn't seem to avoid shocking myself on doorknobs or the stovetop. And my cats simply couldn't understand why touching things—which was, after all, an unavoidable part of everyday life—suddenly meant enduring a tiny, but still startling, twinge of pain. It happened when they touched me, or each other, or brushed up against the metal handle of a kitchen cabinet. And how could they even escape the occasional encounter with a kitchen cabinet, or the hinge of a closet or bathroom door, when there was no furniture for them to rest on or hide under? The lack of anything to perch on—of a comfortable sofa or bed, long-since made their own with scratches and scent marking—was deeply unsettling in and of itself. The heated cat beds made things somewhat easier for all of us. Still, none of us were feeling particularly jazzed about this alarming and seemingly merit-less life change I'd foisted upon us all.

And then, just like that, everything changed.

A couple of days before Valentine's Day, it finally snowed. It wasn't the first time I'd ever seen snow, but—unless you counted a couple of very light dustings while I was in college in Atlanta—it was the first time I'd seen snow in any significant quantities since I was sixteen years old, when a high-school class trip had brought me to Boston in the winter.

Eventually, the snow that had fallen to cover the streets and sidewalks of New York City would turn yellow from dog-walkers and black from muddy boots and car tires, before being shoved into mounds on street corners and hardening into ice piles that made the simple act of crossing on foot at an intersection a difficult endeavor, at best. But, for that first day or two, it was beautiful. It was glorious. It's hard to explain the sheer wonder that a transplanted Miamian feels upon seeing a city like New York blanketed in snow for the first time. The endless, perfect whiteness of it, stretching for miles and miles when viewed from the windows of a high-rise apartment building—the hush that falls over the city, the way that all its hard edges are softened and blurred. The slate-gray of the sky before the snow had turned the entire city the same dulled gray. Now though, for just a day or two, its streets and buildings glowed gently with a kind of pearlescent aura, casting a bright gleam onto the faces of the handful of pedestrians hardy enough to traverse the sidewalks while the snow was still falling, before shovels and snowplows had done their job.

Watching through my windows as the snow fell, in my corner apartment way up on the thirty-first floor, was like being inside a snow globe. Scarlett and Vashti were as enchanted with it as I was. Scarlett climbed to a windowsill and, standing up on her hind legs like a prairie dog, batted her paw gently again and again at the panes of glass, trying to catch the flakes that danced tantalizingly just beyond her reach. She stretched her neck and craned her head to see as far upward as she could, clearly filled with as much wide-eyed wonder as I was as she took in a spectacle that not only hadn't she ever seen before, but had never even known might exist. She sat there for hours with her head turned up and her front paws pressed against the glass, only occasionally looking back over her shoulder at the rest of us. *Does everybody else see this?* she seemed to be asking. *What* is *all this wonderful white stuff?!*

As for Vashti, my arctic fox of a cat, something deep and instinctive within her seemed to recognize the snow instantly. I had my reservations about letting Scarlett and Vashti out onto the small balcony of my apartment (that Homer would *never* go out on that balcony, of course, went without saying). But Vashti ran back and forth between me and the balcony door so anxiously, and with such plaintive squeaks of entreaty, that I couldn't resist her. I put on my old bomber jacket and a pair of rubber galoshes (the closest thing I had to snow boots that winter) and stood shivering on the balcony with her as she plunged deep into the highest drift where the wind had blown the snow against one balcony wall. She leapt and burrowed and tunneled into the snow, the whiteness of her fur disappearing into it so completely that eventually she was only discernible by the contrast her emerald-green eyes and little pink nose made against the white-on-white landscape she created. She wasn't as happy when, upon our reentry indoors, I bundled her up and rubbed her down vigorously with a towel. But then I stepped into the shower myself, turning on the hot water at full blast, and Vashti dozed contentedly atop the clothes hamper in the steamy bathroom, as drowsily contented as an old man taking a *shvitz*.

Homer couldn't see the snow, and so didn't quite understand what all the fuss was about. But the sound of the cold wind outside was stilled for once, muffled by the falling snow, and the rest of us seemed unusually contented—and the ever-empathic Homer picked up on our mood, and was contented himself. I made some instant cocoa in the microwave and poured it into one of the Styrofoam cups I'd been accumulating in my small kitchen until my dishes and glassware finally arrived, then inflated my air mattress and sat, with my cocoa beside me, propped up on my pillows against the wall. Homer climbed into my lap, then burrowed his way beneath the ancient sweatshirt I wore until his small head popped out through the neck—which I'd cut and widened back in my college days (as early-90s fashion had dictated). I gently rubbed Homer's head with one hand, and turned the pages of a book with the other and, for the two or three hours before the air mattress deflated once again, I reveled in the deep warmth of his purr against my chest and neck while the snow fell silently outside. Scarlett and Vashti, having exhausted themselves, slept soundly in their heated cat beds.

Despite having wanted, for almost as long as I could remember, to move to New York, I'd been homesick beyond the telling of it for the past two weeks. "Home," in my mind, still meant Miami. Miami was warm and familiar and easy, whereas everything about New York so far had proven to be cold and strange and just *hard*. I had been embarrassed to admit it to myself, and had never once mentioned the homesickness that churned in the pit of my stomach, night and day, to the family and friends I'd left behind—some of whom, at my going-away party, had predicted that I'd be back within a few months. *Not me*, I'd assured them. *Never.* Faced with the reality of actually living here, though, my certainty had wavered considerably. Still, I was stubborn and proud and felt that I'd rather let myself be drawn and quartered than acknowledge that maybe the naysayers had been right, and that moving to Manhattan had been a colossal mistake.

Now, though—for once—everything here was white and quiet and peaceful and warm. Scarlett, on her back in her little cat bed with all four paws in the air, snored lightly in her sleep. Vashti had positioned herself in her own bed so that she could see the snow on the balcony when she half-opened her eyes from time to time, already imagining further adventures whenever I consented to go out there with her again. But I was in no hurry. The warm weight of Homer lying against my chest beneath my shirt dispelled that ever-present knot of homesickness in the pit of my stomach. I paused in my reading to marvel at the feeling of it being gone, and dropped a kiss on the top of Homer's head.

"You're my good boy," I murmured into his black fur. "You're my good, good boy." And Homer, as warm and contented for the moment as I was, lifted his chin to nuzzle his head into my neck, purring harder.

AFTER THAT, IT WAS as if a fever had broken—a strange, cold sort of fever, to be sure.

The apartment was still chilly and mostly empty, and it didn't take long for the snow outside to turn into an irritating and unappealing slush that even Vashti lost interest in. But the feeling engendered by the moment of grace that had descended on all of us the day it snowed lingered. Whatever feelings of guilt (on my part), of resentment (on the cats' part), or homesickness (on all our parts) had evaporated the way the last traces of that snow eventually would within a few weeks.

It was only two days later—on Valentine's Day, as fate would have it—when my furniture and belongings were finally delivered. Out from the moving van and into my apartment came our bed, our couch, our coffee table, our rugs, our lamps, our plates and silverware and assorted knickknacks. The apartment felt smaller once it was filled, but also infinitely more comfortable. The smell of new paint and varnish gave way to the familiar scent of us, and the life we'd made together over the years.

The best Valentine's Day gift I could have asked for—better than a box of candy or a dozen red roses to display on the desk of my office—was the deep and comfortable sleep I enjoyed that first night when I finally had my own bed back. If I'd had anyone to invite, I might actually have thrown a party to celebrate ditching that wretched air mattress in my building's trash room.

I didn't have anybody who I could have invited to a party then, but eventually I would. Eventually the weather would turn warmer, and I'd befriend coworkers and colleagues. And in August of that year, at the rooftop birthday party for a friend of a friend, I'd end up meeting a hilarious film journalist named Laurence. I didn't even suspect, that first night, that I would end up marrying him someday. But I did know, from the very first time we spoke, that he was the funniest person I'd ever met, and that I wanted to spend as much time with him as I could decently get away with. (He had a girlfriend back then, who I also met that night—but that's a story for another time.)

Things got better, in other words. And I never did end up moving back to Miami, despite some of the pessimistic predictions that certain friends of mine—and that I, myself, in moments of despair—had made.

But before any of that happened, even before the furniture arrived, I'd gotten over the unsettling feeling of homesickness and constant strangeness in this new place. Yes, my new life in New York was new and different, frequently cold and, for a brief time, empty of the familiar things I'd collected over the years. Yet, even still, I realized, I was luckier than most people.

"Home," to me, had never meant a precise place or city or collection of rooms. It wasn't a certain smell or type of climate or a specific piece of furniture.

For me, home was wherever my cats were. And my cats would always come with me, wherever I went. We'd never been the exiles, the vagabonds cast onto the strange shores of a cold and unfamiliar place, that in darker moments I'd imagined us to be.

It had been foolish, I realized, ever to have felt homesick. The four of us had never left our home. We'd been home the whole time.

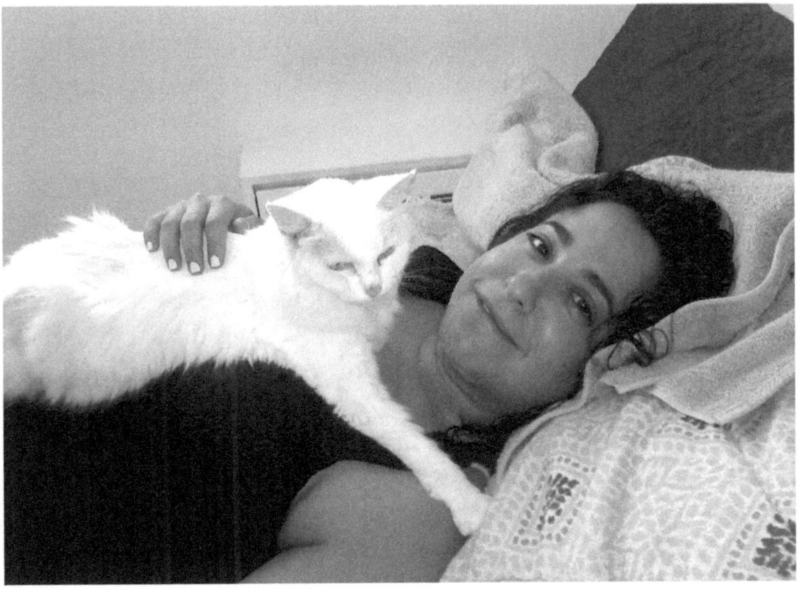

Nothing Bad Ever Happens in Stars Hollow

By the time I finally realized how skinny Vashti had gotten, she'd already crossed the threshold from "maybe a little too skinny" to "definitely and alarmingly underweight." I don't know if realizing how serious the problem was sooner would ultimately have changed anything about the outcome. Nevertheless—and even though it's now ten years later—I still haven't quite forgiven myself.

I can be a pretty ruthless self-prosecutor, so I always try (although I don't always succeed) to mount an equally spirited defense on my own behalf. When it comes to Vashti, that defense is twofold and goes something like this: In the first place, Vashti had so much long, luxurious, beautiful fur that the overall effect was to make her appear plumper than she really was—and not just plumper, but healthier. What reasonable person could have looked at a gorgeous creature like my Vashti and thought "sickly" or "too skinny" or anything other than "absolutely perfect"?

And, in the second place, Vashti had already lost a fair chunk of weight five years earlier when we'd moved in with Laurence, slimming her down enough that her weight loss *now* did not, at first, seem dramatic or even particularly noticeable. It had actually been a *good* thing five years prior, since she'd put on some excess weight in the year or two before. She'd also taken to occasionally neglecting her grooming—possibly made more difficult by her weight gain—and I would have to untangle the silky strands of fur on her back with a comb, lest they otherwise knot into a dirty gray clump that could only be removed with scissors.

Vashti had made it clear in various ways over the years (ways that I've written about in previous stories) that under no circumstances would she tolerate living with anyone but me. And yet, Vashti had always been a cat who, more than anything, craved having a human all to herself—a human who was her very own, who didn't have to be shared with other cats.

I could never have been that person for her. But Laurence could be, and he was. The two of them fell head-over-heels in love with each other, and within only a few months of our moving in with him Vashti had not only lost all the excess weight, she'd resumed grooming herself as meticulously as if she expected photographers might show up unannounced at any moment to snap her picture. A routine physical a few months after the move had turned up nothing unusual in her blood work or anything to be alarmed about. Vashti's renewed energy and general zest for life—the way she devotedly followed Laurence from room to room of our apartment and demanded his attention for spirited games of fetch, and the way she'd begun substituting time in Laurence's lap for those extra visits to the kitchen and demands for treats—were, according to our vet, the likeliest explanation behind Vashti's return to her normal weight.

This was back in 2005. But then one day, in January of 2010, I stroked Vashti's back and realized I could feel her spine. And when I put down a treat on the ground for her, I noticed with alarm that while she appeared interested in it—following the movement of my hands with her eyes and eagerly lowering her snout the moment the treat touched the ground—a fit of sneezing overtook her almost immediately and prevented her from being able to eat it.

Neither of these things could be explained away as "a general zest for life," obviously. Within half an hour, I had Vashti at the vet's office.

It would be another eight days before she returned home.

My grandmother moved in with my family when I was four years old and lived with us until she passed away, at the age of

seventy-two, just before my sixteenth birthday. She'd taken pills daily for her blood pressure and thyroid, self administered routine insulin shots for diabetes, and had undergone physical therapy following a stroke she'd had the summer I was twelve. It was after her stroke, when mundane tasks became more difficult, that I began helping my grandmother with some of the little things with which a twelve-year-old could be safely entrusted, like brushing out her long, black hair at night, and keeping her fingernails and toenails trimmed and polished.

So it wasn't as if I didn't have any firsthand or practical knowledge of the realities of elder care. I already knew that aging inevitably brought with it age-related conditions that often required the regular taking of medication, at a minimum, to mitigate. I knew that older people sometimes needed a little extra assistance, especially following a major physical trauma. Caring for my grandmother at home after she'd returned from the hospital had demanded some work from all of us at first—although at the time we'd just been so thrilled to have her home that it hadn't seemed to matter.

That was easy for me to say, of course. I hadn't *really* been responsible for my grandmother—or her health. I was just a kid. It was my mother who'd determined what needed to be done and then who needed to do which part. She did most of the actual work, and did so more or less behind the scenes. It was only later, as an adult, when I'd been able to look back and realize how much time and effort—and, undoubtedly, how many tears for the mother with whom my own mother had always been extraordinarily close—must have been behind what had seemed, to me at least, to be a seamless effort.

If I'd been thinking clearly while Vashti was in the hospital, in other words, I would have known without having to be told that the odds of my thirteen-year-old cat's returning home in the same perfect health she'd been in the year before—and needing no follow-up care aside from the tons of additional TLC I was already prepared to smother her with—were essentially nil.

But I wasn't thinking clearly. During the week when Vashti was at the hospital, my mind operated in essentially two modes. The first mode was consumed with the agony of being separated from her and the persistent fear that she might never come back to us. This was the mental fog in which I passed the majority of my waking hours.

It was during this time when my publisher asked me for a new Afterword for *Homer's Odyssey*, to be included in the paperback edition that would be released some eight months later in September. I sat down and diligently wrote an update on how all three cats had been doing over the past year—leaving out, of course, any mention of the past few days that Vashti had been in the hospital—and I went through recent pictures of all three cats to include in the Afterword. Here was Vashti enjoying a handmade cat blanket a reader had sent her, and here was Vashti again sniffing at some new toys, and there was Vashti squeezed in next to Homer as the two of them tried to find their way into my lap at the same time. What were the odds that Vashti would even be here in September, when this Afterword was finally published? I worked diligently to get it completed by deadline and then, once I'd emailed everything to my publisher, I got into bed and sobbed for the better part of an hour.

The second mode in which my mind worked that week was the pure joy I felt for the one hour each day that Laurence and I were permitted to spend with Vashti at the animal hospital, watching as she ate with enthusiasm again (something I was immensely grateful to see) before climbing into each of our laps in turn to spend long, purring minutes as she assured us that she missed us, too. Vashti looked and felt plumper, happier, and healthier with every passing day, and I—without thinking about it too hard—simply assumed on some level that, when she was finally permitted to return home with us, things would more or less be the way they'd been before.

I was abruptly disabused of this notion on the eighth day, when Laurence and I finally went to the animal hospital to bring her home.

We were ushered in from the waiting room to the exam room where we'd customarily been left alone with Vashti for our visits during her stay. Today, though, we were greeted by Vashti's vet, who was waiting for us *sans* Vashti and holding a thick stack of papers, which she put into my hands. They were, I quickly realized as I flipped through them, explanations of Vashti's various conditions and the aftercare that would now be required to address them.

I already knew that Vashti had been diagnosed with hyperthyroidism—which accounted for her sudden weight loss, and the effects of which could be almost entirely managed by a lower dosage of the same thyroid medication my grandmother had once taken—and also chronic renal failure. The CRF was, by far, the more serious diagnosis. I didn't fully realize how much more serious, however, until the vet launched into a complicated spiel that laid out in full detail Vashti's new elder-care regimen.

Over the course of the next ten minutes, no fewer than six pill bottles were presented to me, and it was only then that I understood the domino effect Vashti's failing kidneys were having on the rest of her system—although the sheer size of the pill for her kidneys, large enough that it could easily have passed as a horse tranquilizer, and looking like something that even I might have trouble swallowing, would have clued me in to the condition's gravity had I still been in the dark.

I didn't have much time to wonder, however, how I would possibly be able to get both the smallish thyroid pill and the enormous, horse-sized kidney pill down a presumably *very* reluctant Vashti's gullet each and every day before the vet had moved on. The buildup of toxins in Vashti's blood from her improperly functioning kidneys was causing her stomach to fill with acid, which accounted for the "sneezing" I'd noticed when she tried to eat at home (it was actually acid reflux). A daily antacid pill would likely take care of that. The crowding out of nutrients by toxins in Vashti's blood was also causing her heart to work a lot harder, resulting in high blood pressure. The high blood pressure required a pill, as well. Plus, Vashti appeared to be anemic (also contributing to her high blood pressure), a condition that might—or might not!—result from her CRF.

"Which pill treats that?" I asked the vet, looking at what was by now a bewildering array of pill bottles in front of me, and she replied, "That's treated with a daily shot, actually. One of the techs will show you when she teaches you how to give Vashti her daily subcutaneous fluid injections."

So great was my dismay upon hearing that I would have to inject Vashti with not one but two (!!!) needles every single day that I didn't even flinch when the vet placed *yet another* pill bottle before me. "This is an appetite stimulant," she told me. "It's important that Vashti keeps eating her prescription kidney-support food, but she doesn't seem to like it very much. This pill should help with that."

Normally, the news that I would now have to figure out a way at mealtimes to keep Vashti from eating the food I gave the other two cats—and vice versa—would, all by itself, have seemed like an insurmountable obstacle. Maybe somebody out there had a multi-cat household where each cat ate every last bite of his or her own designated food as soon as it was put down—thus precluding another cat in the house from digging into it later—but I, personally, had never lived in such a household. In my house, the cats tended to eat first from one bowl, and then switch around in a complex pattern that I could never quite figure out—although one that clearly made sense to them—until each cat had taken at least a few bites from each of the other cats' bowls, yet also making sure that a few morsels remained in each bowl for later, more leisurely, snacking. Was I going to have to start locking Vashti up at mealtimes like a prisoner in a cell until her bowl was completely cleaned?

I hardly had time to consider that, however, before I felt Laurence's hand on the small of my back, gently propelling me into another room where at last I saw Vashti herself, waiting in her carrier next to one of the animal hospital's vet techs.

I'd read often enough in books about how a character's mind "went numb," and—much as I hate to traffic in clichés—that's pretty much exactly what had happened to me by that point. I watched dully as the vet tech carefully lifted a flailing Vashti from her carrier and forced six pills, one at a time, down her throat, crooning gently and stroking Vashti's throat, to encourage swallowing, as she did so. Vashti resisted as strenuously as a cat can when she's too sweet-natured to use her claws or teeth to fend someone off—although you'd actually be surprised (or maybe you wouldn't) at just how effective a cat's nonviolent resistance can be. The tech's brow was moist with perspiration by the time she was done, I noted with dismay, and I couldn't help wondering how I—an inexperienced non-professional—would ever manage this same feat on my own. "It'll be easier at home if you wrap her up in a towel first with just her head sticking out," the tech cheerfully informed me. "We call it the 'kitty burrito.'"

Vashti was still flipping and heaving in the vet tech's hands as the tech carefully placed her belly down on the exam table, ran her hand down Vashti's back a few times to calm her, then produced an array of needles. She carefully loaded a few CCs of Vashti's anemia medication into one of the hypodermics. "You should make a little 'tent' from the skin on the back of her neck like this," the tech told me, using three fingers to produce a triangle of loose flesh where Vashti's head met her body, "and then just ease the needle in very gently like this." Vashti jumped a little when the needle entered, but didn't yelp. "They hardly have any nerve endings back there," the tech assured me, "so she shouldn't really feel it much. And then to give her her subcutaneous fluid injections every day you just attach one of these needles to the end of this tube..." Here the vet tech produced an IV drip bag filled with saline solution, swiftly and expertly affixing a needle to the end of the drip tube that ran from it. "Then just make the skin tent on the back of her neck again, gently insert the needle, and hold the bag up and the cat down until the fluid in the bag hits this line," she indicated one of the measuring lines on the saline-solution bag. "Then you discard the needle, seal off the drip like so, and put it away for next time."

By this time, I could barely hear the vet tech—or anything happening around me—through the muted buzzing sound that filled the space between my ears. I was still trying to figure out how she'd managed to hold Vashti's entire body in place with nothing more than the three fingers that were making the "skin tent" on the back of Vashti's neck.

Just about the only thing I was consciously aware of was the matter-of-fact voice in my head assuring me that there was no way on God's green earth I would be able to do *any*—much less *all*—of this at home myself. And that, as a direct result of my incompetence, Vashti would certainly die.

THE SORT OF FUGUE state that I'd begun to enter standing there in the vet's office threatened to grow into full-blown catatonia over the next few days. Having Vashti home again was far from the joyous experience I'd been envisioning while she was gone. It wasn't that I minded the work of caring for her—at least, not in theory. But in reality I was proving to be so inept—so wholly unequal to the task—that my ineptitude threatened not only my cat's health and well-being, but also my entire sense of who I was as a person. *The kind of person who'd let a cat die in her care, that's who,* a voice in my head coldly informed me hundreds of times each day.

I had broken the administering of Vashti's six pills into three two-pill sessions stretched out over the course of the day. This had seemed to make sense, as it was literally impossible for me to get six pills down Vashti's throat all at once. Heck, it was essentially impossible for me to get even *two* pills down her throat.

The "kitty burrito" did keep Vashti from flailing around while I tried to pill her, but getting Vashti wrapped up in a bath towel was its own challenge. It got so that any time I picked up anything made of terrycloth, even a tiny dishtowel, Vashti would eye me warily—and if she saw me headed toward her with anything larger, she'd be on her feet and off in a sprint before I knew it. She was surprisingly spry for a cat who'd been practically at death's door less than two weeks earlier, and I *always* had to chase her around the couch and coffee table a few times before she made it to the hallway, at which point either a) Laurence would pop out of his home office in time to grab her, or b) she'd make it to the master bedroom and would be under the bed—and essentially untouchable—before I could reach her. At which point I'd have to wait at least an hour before she emerged and we could start the whole process over again.

But even when I did manage to get Vashti firmly swaddled in a bath towel, it was still only a minimally effective technique to use on a cat determined to spit out pills at all costs. "I can be just as stubborn as you," I'd tell her, through gritted teeth, clutching a be-toweled Vashti to my chest for five minutes or longer, holding her jaws closed with one hand and stroking her throat with the other (to encourage swallowing) until it seemed physically impossible for her not to have swallowed the pills by now—only to discover, as two sodden half-pills came whizzing out of Vashti's mouth the moment I released her, that when it comes to stubbornness, it's exceedingly rare for a human to be able to best a cat.

Greenies Pill Pockets, recommended by my vet, were a big hit and seemed to do the trick at first—that is, until I realized that Vashti was eating the Pill Pocket *around* the pill and spitting out the pill itself. I used to find mangled, spat-out, and vomited-up—yet nevertheless frustratingly intact—pills lying all over the house those first few days. After a week, I gave up on the horse-sized kidney pill altogether, hoping that the achieving of smaller, more attainable goals—like getting Vashti to swallow her relatively tiny antacid and thyroid pills—would create the momentum necessary for me to tackle bigger tasks (and bigger pills). But I couldn't even get that far, and so the momentum never came.

And then there were the injections! The anemia shot wasn't so bad—I'd sit cross-legged on the floor, pull Vashti close, and put a couple of treats on one leg; then, while she was distracted by the treats, I'd slip the hypodermic into the back of her neck with no problem. But the subcutaneous fluid injections were much rougher going. On the second and third days I drew blood as I kept trying—with little success—to slip the larger IV-drip needle easily into the back of Vashti's neck. Laurence gently held her down atop an enormous gold-velvet cushion on the bedroom floor while I fumbled with the needle and Vashti turned huge, miserable eyes my way before she jumped in pain. When I saw the smear of blood against the white fur on the nape of her neck, I literally—*literal-*

ly—wanted to die. I had hurt my cat. *I had hurt Vashti.* I'd *drawn blood* from an injury that I, myself, had inflicted upon her.

It's difficult even now for me to put into words how hard that was for me to cope with, or how nearly impossible it was to force myself to try again the next day—my hands shaking so hard with the fear that I might hurt her once more that injuring her became a near certainty.

When I didn't feel anguished, I wasn't feeling anything at all other than numb. And when I wasn't caring for Vashti, I barely got off the couch except to shuffle to and from the bedroom or bathroom at regular intervals. I had stopped changing out of sweatpants, eating at regular intervals, and even routine bathing and hygiene was becoming a thing of the past. The only one who seemed to appreciate how much more…intense…my personal odor had become was Homer, who twitched his little nose a few times and then, with what appeared to be great satisfaction, nestled against my chest and into the sweatshirt I'd been wearing for the better part of nearly a week.

Weighing me down wasn't simply the realization of my own inadequacy to rise to the challenge of this particular moment—although that was bad enough. But mixed in with that was the realization that my cats were now officially old enough to begin experiencing the illnesses of old age—which therefore meant that I was now entering the phase of my life when I would begin to lose them. I'd almost lost Vashti already and didn't know how much longer she'd be with me. (*Not very long at all if you can't get more than the occasional half-pill into her*, the mean voice in my head predicted.)

I did know, though, that this illness would be her final illness.

Those were dark days. And even now, as I look back, I'm honestly not sure that I would have made it through the cold, bleak January of 2010 if not for the discovery of what I came to refer to as "television Prozac."

Relief for my bruised and aching spirit came in the form of a ten-year-old WB dramedy known as *Gilmore Girls*.

I'd heard about the show for years, although I'd never seen so much as a single episode. As it happened, however, that first Monday when Vashti was at the hospital, ABC Family began airing *Gilmore Girls* reruns one hour a day, five days a week, starting from the very first episode. Flipping channels randomly that Monday, I came upon the pilot episode and dimly recalled that there was a smallish, but nevertheless fervent, cult following of *Gilmore Girls* enthusiasts out there, and figured, *Why not?*

There are probably junkies who didn't fall as hard or fast for heroin as I fell for *Gilmore Girls*. It very quickly got to the point where that hour when I got my "fix" became the only reliably painless sixty-minute stretch of my entire day.

As you probably already know, *Gilmore Girls* was a WB show about a 32-year-old woman—the beautiful only child of a wealthy family—who got pregnant at 16, decided to raise the baby, and who wound up some sixteen years later in possession of an adorable little house, the head manager of an equally adorable little inn (where her very best friend is head chef), and the mother of a beautiful, brilliant, reasonably well-adjusted sixteen-year-old daughter. The two Gilmore girls—mother Lorelei and namesake daughter Rory (for short)—navigate the ups and downs of life and love and school and friendships and careers armed with fabulous clothes, a dazzlingly quick wit, and the unshakeable bond they share with each other.

Did I mention that both Gilmore girls can—and do!—eat anything and everything they want without gaining a single ounce?

Years before I actually saw the show, I'd once read an article that described *Gilmore Girls* as being pure, borderline pornographic, female wish fulfillment. I think that assessment is about right. Not that most women are dying to become unwed teenage mothers, of course. Nevertheless, there's an undeniable appeal to the idea of having a child when you're young enough to get your figure back immediately afterward—and to still be young enough (barely in your mid-30s!) to have an entirely new and fulfilling post-child-rearing life when that child finally leaves the nest. To get to make all parenting decisions yourself without having to consult or argue with a co-parent about them. To have a job where you're the boss and get to see your best friend every day. To have enough money to keep yourself and your daughter in an endless array of cute clothes and dinners out (Lorelei Gilmore literally never prepares dinner once over the entire seven-year run of the show), and to also have rich parents to fall back on if things ever get *really* dicey. And last, but certainly not least, to have a teenaged daughter—a Yale-bound class valedictorian, mind you—who views you as her closest friend and wisest, most trusted confidant.

Watching that show, there were moments when—hand to God—I actually fleetingly regretted that I hadn't allowed my high school boyfriend to knock me up. (Although at the time it had seemed like an eminently responsible choice.)

Re-reading this now makes me slightly embarrassed to admit just how hard I fell for the show. But, truth be told, it wasn't Lorelei and Rory who I was most infatuated with. It was with the aggressively quaint, cozy-yet-quirky small town of Stars Hollow, Connecticut—where Lorelei and Rory made their home after Lorelei had fled her parents' house with an infant Rory in tow—that I found myself irretrievably in love.

Day after day—while Vashti was gone and then when she first came back home—found me lying on the couch, watching and re-watching the precious few episodes of *Gilmore Girls* I'd managed to DVR thus far. A certain amount of magical thinking set in, so that I'm pretty sure I was convinced on some deep-seated, albeit totally irrational, level that if I watched those episodes long enough, I might actually be transported into Stars Hollow myself.

I re-watched the episodes so frequently, in fact, that Laurence finally called a friend at Warner Brothers and had them send me the box set of the whole series. Suddenly, I found myself the unimaginably rich possessor of forty-two discs and seven entire seasons of snappy dialogue and bucolic, small-town charm.

"You really love that show" Laurence observed, as I recklessly tore through packaging and shrink-wrap before gently, almost reverently, withdrawing a Season 2 disc and inserting it into the DVR.

"Nothing bad ever happens in Stars Hollow," I replied.

And it was true. Everything—*everything*—felt bad in my life right at that moment. But nothing bad ever happened in Stars Hollow. New York City in January was relentlessly cold and dark and utterly cheerless, but Stars Hollow—no matter what time of year it was in any particular episode—was endlessly warm and welcoming. There were certainly no lingering, complex, potentially fatal illnesses—nor any caregivers being ground down by their own inability to minister to someone they loved.

Perhaps the best way to describe the fictional town of Stars Hollow is to say that it was like the small town in a cozy mystery series except without any murders. It was the kind of town where the seasons always arrived pitch-perfect and precisely on cue. The autumns were perfectly autumnal and began punctually in early October with neither too much nor too little red, amber, orange, or russet in the leaves of the trees. No Stars Hollow local was ever heard to say something like, "We had such a dry summer—that's why the trees are dull this year," because something like less-than-glorious fall foliage would never happen in Stars Hollow. Stars Hollows winters were always warmed by hot chocolate with marshmallows and accented by virgin-white snow that never hardened into dirty brown ice after being kicked around by car tires for a couple of weeks. (People in Stars Hollow walked everywhere, and all that exercise is probably why residents were generally of above-average attractiveness.) Spring in Stars Hollow was always greeted by the blooming of Technicolor flowers, and in the summer the trees burst into glorious green leaf. And some thoughtful person, at some point, had strung all those trees with fairy lights that twinkled tastefully, yet merrily, all year round.

Stars Hollow denizens were a bit off-kilter, to be sure—eccentric individualists prone to comical grievances and the occasional squabble, which was only to be expected in a town that prided itself on having played some murkily defined role in the Revolutionary War. But the townspeople were also, to a man, funny, warm, close-knit, and *there*. No wonder problems never seemed to drag on past the single televised hour in which they were introduced—with a veritable army of loving, if somewhat daffy, well-wishers to help out, how could hardships possibly linger?

I'd once lived in a picturesque small town myself. Although South Beach was technically a part of Miami Beach—which was itself a subsidiary of the Greater Miami metropolitan area—it was also an island community measuring only one square mile in size, and those of us who lived there back in the Nineties and early Aughts tended to think of ourselves as being sealed off from the rest of Miami and the world beyond it, only open to outsiders insofar as we welcomed their tourist dollars. Of course, being a town in the real world, South Beach had its real-world problems—something I was reminded of as I was unburdening myself over the phone to a close friend from those days—a friend who was now coming up on his tenth anniversary in Narcotics Anonymous.

"Pills are the worst," my friend told me, sympathizing wholly with Vashti. "That's why I always ground mine up and snorted them."

It was an honest-to-gosh lightbulb moment for me. *It's so simple*, I marveled, feeling a giddy little tingle that was the closest thing to actual happiness I'd felt in nearly three weeks. *Why didn't I think of it sooner?!!?*

That very afternoon, I showered, dressed in clothing that wasn't fancy but also wasn't sweatpants, and actually ventured out of our apartment—first to a high-end cooking supplies store, where I obtained a porcelain mortar and pestle, and then back to the vet's office, where I picked up a package of plastic syringes. As soon as I got home, I used my new mortar and pestle to grind all six of Vashti's pills into a fine powder. I then mixed the powdered pills with a little bit of water, loaded the concoction into one of the syringes, scooped a napping Vashti up in one arm, and with my free hand wedged the syringe between Vashti's jaws. Quick as you please, I shot the liquid through her lips and down her throat before she even realized what was happening.

Vashti had started squirming the moment the syringe touched her mouth, and she eyed me balefully now as she walked off in a sulk—sputtering and spitting, yet unable to disgorge any of the medication she'd already reflexively swallowed.

I, on the other hand, was feeling something close to euphoria. I'd gotten six pills into my cat in under six seconds. It seemed like a miracle.

True, I'd never be able to catch Vashti quite so unawares again. As the weeks went by, I found that I still had to get her into the "kitty burrito," and that if I didn't angle the syringe just right, she'd be apt to foam and spit until a significant portion of the liquid came back up.

By and large, though, our once-daily pilling sessions (down from three!) were essentially problem free. Just about the only hiccup was that I couldn't feed Vashti for a full hour after medicating her—even though her appetite stimulant kicked in much more quickly than that. She'd stand on the kitchen table staring fixedly at me for a good forty-five minutes every day, mutely demanding that I feed her *NOW!* On the downside, this was always an intensely uncomfortable forty-five minutes—so uncomfortable that not even an episode of *Gilmore Girls* could put me entirely at ease. But on the upside, Vashti was so ravenous by the time I *did* feed her—on the kitchen table, well away from where the other two cats ate but not locked in a room by herself—that she polished everything off in minutes, which solved the problem of keeping the other cats away from her prescription food and vice versa.

As for the subcutaneous fluid injections, I also got by with a little help from my friends. The warmly sympathetic, infinitely wise, and unquestionably more experienced cat-loving crowd who hung out with me on social media in the early days, before the paperback of *Homer's Odyssey* was published, were—much like the residents of Stars Hollow—quirky and clannish. They loved silly cat memes and cat videos, and spoke in a distinct jargon comprised of words like "pawsitive" and "furiend," which probably would have been difficult for anyone outside our community to grasp at first.

But they were also an eminently practical bunch, and they were the ones who first clued me in to the smaller-gauge needles for SubQ injections than the ones my vet had initially given me (in my ignorance, I hadn't even know that the needles came in different sizes). True, the smaller needles lengthened the amount of time that it took for the fluid to finish dripping from its pouch and into my cat. Yet they made the actual insertion of the needle into the flesh of her neck so completely painless as to be well worth it.

Another online friend with a CRF cat of his own advised me to try heating the fluid to body temperature before dispensing it—a piece of advice so sage that I once again wondered how it had never occurred to me. Of *course* the sensation of warm water flowing through my now perpetually dehydrated Vashti's body would feel much, *much* better than the creepy-crawly feeling of cold water moving directly under her skin. It actually got to the point that Vashti *enjoyed* her SubQ injections, seeming to view them as a sort of daily spa treatment. You could almost hear her thinking, *Ahhhhhhhhhhhhhh...*as her whole body relaxed under Laurence's hands—Laurence always cradled her in his arms while I inserted the needle and dispensed the fluid—and she turned a heavy-lidded look of bliss in my direction. *That feels sooooooo gooooooooood...*

Even if I'd somehow gotten my wish and been able to step into the world of *Gilmore Girls* and Stars Hollow, things couldn't have worked out better—and I wouldn't have been able to find a better circle of friendship and practical support to come to my aid. And, as the gray winter slowly gave way to spring, my own world began once again to blossom into a lavish, Technicolor spring.

🐾 🐾

EVEN IN STARS HOLLOW, cats couldn't live forever. There was a cat in the town named Cinnamon—belonging to a character played by Archie Bunker's daughter—who passed away peacefully in her sleep at a very old age in the Season 1 episode "Cinnamon's Wake." The entire town gathered at the home of Cinnamon's grieving "mom" to comfort her with food, music, funny stories, and fond reminiscences. My tears flowed copiously as I watched that episode and looked over at my own feline brood. Only on TV, I thought, could the mourning of a cat's passing, and a celebration of a cat's life, play out as beautifully as it did in Stars Hollow.

A bit of TV magic came to our own lives that April, when a crew from Animal Planet's *Cats 101* spent a day with us to record our cats for an upcoming episode. It was Homer who they were primarily interested in, naturally enough, but they wanted at least a few shots of Scarlett and Vashti as well.

I was apprehensive about the whole thing. By then, Vashti seemed to be doing exceptionally well. She hadn't re-gained all the weight she'd lost—and she never would—but she'd gained back most of it. She ate without difficulty, even played a bit from time to time, and cuddled with us constantly. And, it goes without saying, she looked unbelievably gorgeous. If ever a cat had been born to be on camera, it was my Vashti-girl.

And yet, like anybody caring for an invalid, I worried that the stress and excitement might be too much for her. So I was resistant at first, but finally reached an agreement with the show's producers: One single cameraman, all be himself—with no lighting team or directors or producers or anyone else—would be allowed to come in first thing that morning for thirty minutes to record Scarlett and Vashti, *if Vashti felt up to it*, before the two cats would then retire to the bedroom and spend the rest of the day in undisturbed seclusion.

It was October before our episode aired, and by then Vashti had been gone for nearly two months. Laurence and I were eager to see our cats on TV, of course, but we were also apprehensive. Our grief at Vashti's passing still felt a little raw. We weren't sure if seeing her as she'd once been, only a few months earlier, would be more than we could bear.

We shouldn't have worried. The cameraman who'd come to our home that day had clearly been the last in the long, long line of men who'd fallen for Vashti over the years. He'd shot her beautifully, with several long, lingering close-ups on her lovely face. Vashti's presence, so sorely missed from our home for the last two months, exploded into our living room once again—her enormous green eyes and little pink pearl of a nose larger than life as they filled the entire TV screen for a moment before we saw a brief shot her eating, and then a shot of her trotting away from the living room on her dainty little paws. Laurence and I were holding each other's hands by then, tears in our eyes, as Vashti paused to look directly into the camera—directly at us, or so it felt—one last time before disappearing into the bedroom and out of view.

For a moment—for just that one moment—it was as if Vashti had been resurrected just long enough to visit with us one last time. It was a far greater gift than we'd realized back in April that it would be. And it was hard to imagine that anyone else could ever feel as grateful or as lucky as Laurence and I did in that moment.

Not even in Stars Hollow.

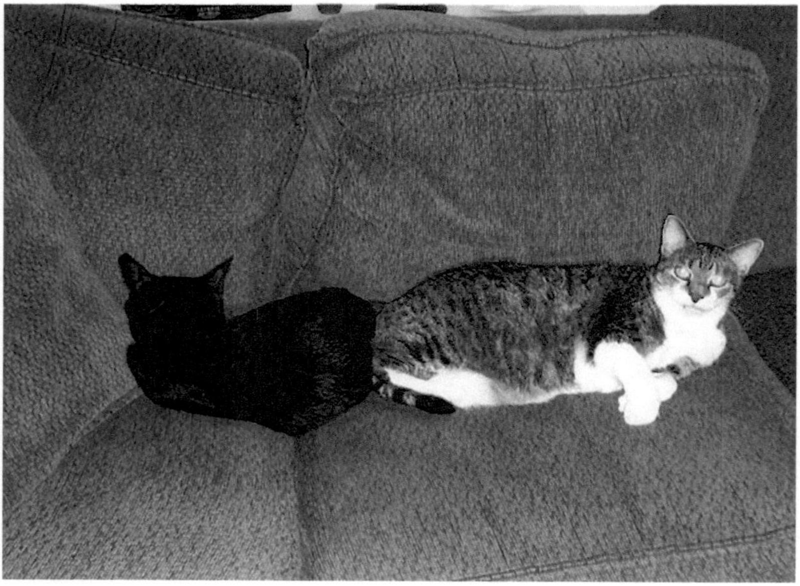

Homer Returns

EVERY SO OFTEN YOU'LL hear about a "breakout character" in a TV show—some minor foil who was originally intended to appear in an episode or two, but to whom viewers have such a strong and positive reaction that the show's writers expand her storyline from one-off to recurring, or from recurring to series regular, or perhaps even to a spin-off show of her very own. Frasier Crane, originally of *Cheers,* is a great example. Another is Mork, a one-off *Happy Days* novelty before landing *Mork and Mindy. All in the Family* begat *Maude* and *Maude* begat *Good Times*, which centered on the family of Maude's housekeeper, Florida. Saul Goodman, for *Better Call Saul*'s sheer virtuosity, may be one of the strongest contenders in this category.

If an inanimate object can be considered a "character," then I inadvertently created just such a breakout character in *Homer's Odyssey*: a little stuffed worm made up of three fluffy balls of cotton yarn (one yellow, one orange, and one green) with a small bell attached to one end. I believe that, at one point, the opposite end featured two glued-on felt eyes to accompany its sewn-on smile. But memory is a chancy thing and tends to become blurrier the farther back you try to reach. If the worm ever did have eyes, they went missing so early that I can't be positive my memory of them is true.

The stuffed worm became a generational hand-me-down of sorts in my little cat family. I had first bought it for Scarlett, and of the many toys I attempted to bribe her affections with in our early days together, it was the only one she showed any consistent interest in. When we adopted Vashti a year later, she immediately laid claim to it herself. I don't know if it can be said that Scarlett relinquished the toy worm with good grace—her interest in it had waned as she'd gotten older, although once Vashti showed a liking for the toy, of course Scarlett decided she'd loved it all along. But, after a handful of tussles and a few token efforts at reclaiming it, eventually she left it for the new kitten.

The worm was already somewhat woebegone by the time Homer came to us a year after Vashti did, the cotton yarn that composed its torso having been teased out into loops, here and there, by playful feline claws. This didn't seem to bother Homer, however. Whether it was the worm's by-then eyelessness (which Homer couldn't really have known about) or the merrily ringing bell in its tail (which Homer most definitely *did* recognize and love), he was instantly charmed by the toy. He took it from Vashti—who parted with it far more benignly than Scarlett had—and cherished it for the next thirteen years.

Neither of Homer's big sisters was ever as rambunctious as Homer was, and there were only so many of Homer's high-spirited hijinks that that they'd voluntarily participate in. But the toy worm was always up for an adventure, a forever-willing playmate and co-conspirator. It became his constant companion, his partner in crime, the co-star in all the thrilling adventure stories that Homer loved to act out—the Sundance Kid to his Butch Cassidy, the Jimmy Olsen to his Superman, the Luca Brasi to his Don Corleone. (That last one, admittedly, may be a stretch; as far as I know, Homer and his stuffed worm never had any trouble with the Feds.)

Its stitched-on smile would beam as brightly the tenth time Homer used his mouth to toss it high in the air as it did the first, and the bell in its tail—which made an excellent homing device for a sightless cat—would tinkle just as cheerfully each and every time it hit the ground. It would patiently "hide" alongside Homer—who usually did so in plain sight, the nuances of hide-and-seek being somewhat fuzzy for a blind cat—whenever he tried to catch one of his sisters in a "surprise" attack. And if Homer decided to sneak up on the worm itself, the worm never once made Homer feel that there was anything fundamentally wrong with his directly-from-the-front assaults—unlike Scarlett, whose ever-ready instructional/retaliatory front paw let Homer know, in no uncertain terms, that hide-and-seek was a game at which he was utterly hopeless.

The worm never objected to filling the role of sidekick or second fiddle. When Homer wanted to play Mighty Big-Cat Hunter, it was perfectly content to be dangled by its neck from his mouth, dragging between his front paws, like some impressive beast that Homer had managed to overpower all by himself through sheer pluck and ingenuity. Or, if Homer was more inclined to play rescuer than hunter, the worm would remain unresisting in one spot until Homer leapt to its aid and carried it to safety, away from whatever dastardly menaces he'd dreamed up to fight off that day. And when the day's play was done, the worm would nestle happily—sticky with cat spittle and scruffy with love—beneath Homer's cheek for a long, companionable nap.

We moved six times over the course of Homer's life and, at each new home, the toy worm was always the first thing Homer sought out when I unpacked the bag or box in which cat supplies had been transported. When we moved to New York from Miami—and Homer flew on a plane with me for the first (and last) time—I bundled Homer and his little toy worm into his carrier together, feeling that having a soft and familiar "buddy" riding alongside him might help alleviate some of the inevitable anxiety a blind cat would feel under such unusual circumstances. Homer ended up being miserable the entire trip anyway (ears as sensitive as Homer's don't fare well on airplanes). Nevertheless, the first thing Homer did, upon being released from his carrier in his new northern home, was to pull the worm out behind him, holding it carefully aloft in his jaws as he methodically explored this unfamiliar space and sought out a safe repository for his most cherished possession.

Homer was nearly twelve years old by the time I sat down to write *Homer's Odyssey*, and I wrote this favored toy—such an integral component of Homer's day-to-day life—into the story. It was impossible not to. Trying to write Homer without his beloved inanimate companion would have been like trying to write Linus from *Peanuts* without his omnipresent security blanket.

Still, I was unprepared for how popular that little stuffed worm became among the book's readers. I received first dozens, then hundreds of emails wanting to know whether Homer still had the worm, whether I had pictures of the two of them together—or even just of the worm, by itself—that I could send to them. They wanted to know about the worm's "health," whether it seemed likely that it would "live" as long as Homer did, and what new adventures the two of them had gotten into together since *Homer's Odyssey* had been published.

One of the things you always have to remember as a writer is that your own opinions regarding your work really only matter up to the point when your book is published. Once it's given over to the public, it's up to them to decide what's good or bad, important or unimportant. Readers have a way of disliking characters you'd loved intensely while writing them, or of finding deep meaning in details that you'd thought of as little more than dashes of color, intended only to flesh out the background of a scene.

So while I, personally, had never thought of Homer's toy worm as being anything more than my main character's prop—much less a breakout star in its own right—once the reading public got hold of him, that's exactly what he became. (And, having acknowledged as much, I now feel obligated to refer to "it" as "him.") The worm became so popular that I even briefly toyed with the idea of giving him his own "spin-off." Perhaps an illustrated children's book about the adventures of Homer and his toy worm—two buckaroos and best pals, side by side, going off on a series of glorious, Technicolor adventures together.

By then, though, the worm was a pitifully bedraggled thing. Only two of the original three cottony puffs were left—the smiling green head, in search of greener pastures, having detached itself from the rest of the body some two years back, never to be heard from again. The remaining orange and yellow puffs were encrusted with the kind of years-long accumulation of grime that not even a thorough laundering could remove entirely. The four metal prongs that closed the worm's bell and made his tail ring out so jauntily had somehow pried themselves open. Now the bell didn't ring so much as make a hollow clunking sound when it struck the ground. Even worse, these days the metal prongs faced outward instead of curling inward, and their sharp edges made for the occasional nasty surprise if I happened to step on the worm unawares while getting out of bed in the morning. It was only a matter of time, I knew, before those sharp, gaping prongs did real damage to a cat or a human, or both.

Intense loyalty was one of Homer's defining trademarks. Even as the worm grew, day by day, to be less like a plaything and more like a tiny four-pronged switchblade with a grungy yarn hilt, Homer clung to him tenaciously.

The inevitable time came, however—at more than fifteen years of age, having long outlived whatever life expectancy his manufacturer had intended him to have—when there was so little of him left that the worm had to go.

THERE PROBABLY NEVER WOULD have been a *good* time for Homer to lose his favorite toy, treasured since his earliest kittenhood. Humans, I learned, aren't the only ones who attach intense emotional freight to inanimate objects, forcing them to bear the weight of cherished memories and younger days gone by. We're not alone in our tendency to love things deeply that will never have the capacity to love us back.

Having to say goodbye to the worm, however, only a few weeks after we'd lost Vashti seemed like an especially cruel blow.

Vashti had always been something of a buffer between Homer and Scarlett, though Homer himself was probably unaware of this. Homer thought, until the very end, that he and Scarlett were the best of friends. To not only catch up to Scarlett, who always fled directly upon picking up Homer's unwitting visual cues that a pounce was imminent—the low crouch, the wiggling backside, the silent, stealthy approach made in full view of everyone—but to pin her down in play and definitively *best* her was the unfulfilled dream of Homer's life. But even without the advantages that sight gave Scarlett, this would have been a challenge. She was the largest of my three cats—at thirteen pounds, nearly three times Homer's size—and the force of her personality, aloof and unyielding as iron, cast an even longer shadow than her physical bulk. Once Scarlett had decreed that playtime was over, the other two cats knew from long and painful experience that no appeals would tempt her back into a game, and there was nothing to be done except find some way to entertain themselves without her.

For all his high energy and big-cat-predator pretensions, Homer didn't have an ounce of malice or genuine dislike in him. So foreign were those traits to his personality, he didn't even know how to recognize them in others. When Homer swatted at Scarlett, he did so in play—and he assumed that she was also playing when she swatted back at him, even if she had an uncomfortable tendency to unsheathe her claws. That's just how Scarlett was, Homer surely thought. That's just what their relationship was—two lifelong buddies in an endless game of tag that didn't need to be won by either in order to be great fun.

Scarlett herself did not share this opinion. Just about everything in life annoyed Scarlett at least a little—the very oxygen she breathed to stay alive only barely tolerated by virtue of its necessity—but the thing that annoyed her most of all was Homer.

All Homer ever wanted was to play with someone. All Scarlett ever wanted was to be left alone. Therefore the two of them were, to a certain extent, at perpetual cross-purposes. But the fact that Scarlett would flee and resist, would swipe at him with her claws and wrestle with him just long enough to show him who was boss, was what made her such an enticing playmate for Homer in the first place. He was always looking for a foe to triumph over, a challenge to overcome. Vashti was too gentle and patient, too apt to let Homer have his own way without putting up any kind of a fight. Where was the fun in that?

Still, Vashti was *there*, and her presence was a kind of safety valve that kept tensions from escalating to the point of no return. After Homer had chased Scarlett around for a while—until she'd whacked him in the face hard enough to indicate with finality: *The game is over*—he could come down off his not-quite-fulfilled high by taking a few swipes at Vashti. Vashti would submit patiently, offering a few affectionate licks to the cheek that Scarlett had just slapped so remorselessly. Homer could then maul his toy worm for a while and, his excess energy expended for the time being, curl up with the worm for a long snooze.

But now Vashti wasn't here anymore. The safety valve was gone. And with the toy worm gone as well, Homer found himself dangerously low on appropriate outlets for the full force of his playfulness. Suddenly, Scarlett was faced with bearing the entire brunt of it all on her own.

If I'd been paying closer attention, I might have seen the crisis that was brewing right underneath my nose. But I was dealing with my own grief. And while I'd had a sense ahead of time of how hard it would be to lose Vashti—something I'd been forced to think about almost daily during the nine long months that she and I had battled her chronic renal failure together—I still wasn't prepared for the full, body-blow force of it when it finally happened.

Laurence likes to say that if you live in New York long enough, you look around one day and realize that everyone on the subway is younger than you are. Clinging to a pole on the 6 train one afternoon about a week after we'd lost Vashti—at a moment when my iPod, set to "shuffle songs" and in a bit of unfortunate timing, presented me with "Landslide" by Fleetwood Mac—I felt a swift and awful gut punch of pain so intense that I doubled over, and a girl in her twenties who was seated nearby immediately jumped up to offer me her seat.

I was only a year shy of my fortieth birthday. I may not have been the oldest person in that subway car, but I was far from being the youngest—or even among the youngest. I had adopted Scarlett, Vashti, and Homer when they were wee kittens and I was still in my early twenties, barely out of college and only halfway launched into what would eventually be my adult life. Now I was nearly forty. I was nearly forty and I'd just lost the first of my three cats—the cats of my youth—to old age. And the swift certainty that hit me in that moment on the train wasn't just that the four of us would never—not ever, not even one more time in all the time to come—be together again.

It was that we would never be young together again.

I won't put my thoughts into Homer's head and say that he felt the same way I did. But, acknowledged or not, the passage of years and the changes that come with it are both inevitable and inexorable for us all. At thirteen, Homer was far older in "cat years" than I was in human ones. Of the three beloved companions of his youth—Scarlett, Vashti, and that silly, tattered little toy worm—time had taken two of them already, one swiftly upon the heels of the other. Homer had never known—had never, in all his thirteen years, even suspected—that someone you loved with your whole heart could just up and leave you one day and never come back. The suddenness of the change must have been disorienting for him in ways that I could no more fully understand than he could fully understand my own feelings.

Grief has a way of making us selfish. I had tried to give my cats extra attention, in the form of treats and cuddles, after Vashti was gone, assuming they must have felt a general sadness that was similar to, if still less than, my own. But I didn't stop to think deeply about how painful and confusing it all must have been for Homer—for Homer and Scarlett both, and not just for me.

I didn't think about it until a few days after that subway ride, when I found my two remaining cats engaged in what gave every indication of being a knock-down, drag-out, and utterly serious battle to the death.

IT WAS A WEDNESDAY afternoon in early September and I was home alone, sitting in the bedroom and going through my copy of *Homer's Odyssey* to make notes for an upcoming reading at Blind Cat Rescue in North Carolina. I had just put down my pen and picked up a glass of water from the night table when I heard it. It was the sound of a cat screaming, and it was coming from the living room.

It was a piercing, gut-wrenching, terrifying sound—a sound that I'd never heard before in my life, and certainly not in my own home. Nevertheless, I instantly identified it as Scarlett. Dropping my book but still clutching my glass of water—for no reason other than not wanting to invest the extra second it would have taken to make sure the glass was far enough from the edge of the night table not to topple off it—I ran for the living room. The sight that greeted me was one that would have been, only moments earlier, unimaginable.

Homer and Scarlett were locked together in a ball of teeth, fur, and claws, rolling around and around the living room rug, their jaws at each other's ears and throats. Scattered all around them, and flying up into the air even as I watched, were little tufts of Scarlett's gray and Homer's black fur. Scarlett screamed again, and Homer growled with an anger I hadn't heard from him since that long-ago night in Miami when our apartment had been broken into.

"Hey!" I shouted. "*HEY! STOP IT!!!*" I yelled so loudly that my throat immediately flared up in pain. "*STOP IT RIGHT NOW!!!*" But I might as well have saved the strain on my vocal cords for all the good my shouting did. It was as if Homer and Scarlett hadn't heard me. (Although, as the descendant of a long line of barrel-chested Jewish yellers, I was pretty sure even our neighbors down the hall had heard me.)

Never before had I yelled like that at my cats without having them instantly stop whatever dangerous thing they were doing that had made me yell in the first place—and never before, until this moment, had I felt so utterly helpless where my cats were concerned.

As they continued to tumble over each other in a vicious, snarling embrace, I knew that something bad was about to happen—that something bad *was happening already*. At least one of them was about to get hurt, perhaps seriously. And even though I was standing *right there*, I couldn't stop it.

It took less than a second for my feeling of helplessness to become terror, and for terror to morph into a kind of hyper-adrenalized, clear-headed rage. Moving swiftly until I was nearly on top of them, I dumped the ice water from the glass I still held directly onto Scarlett and Homer. I'd never been one to discipline my cats with a spray bottle of water, and this might have been the first time that they'd ever been good and soaked. So I was expecting the cold water to have the immediate effect of causing them to spring apart from each other in alarm.

But it didn't. It didn't have any effect at all. And I realized then what I had to do.

As I later explained it to Laurence, if you're going to break up a fight between two drunks in a bar by actually getting into the middle of the brawl to separate them, you should go in prepared to catch a punch yourself. So when I decided to reach my arm into the crazed tangle of teeth and claws that had been—only minutes ago—my two beloved and thoroughly trusted cats, I knew that it wasn't a *great* idea while also acknowledging that it was the *only* idea likely to put an end to this before anything irreparable occurred. I was still the biggest one of the three of us, after all. Nobody was better equipped than I was to play the role of bouncer.

Bracing myself, I plunged my arm into the frenzied jumble of cats. My hand took an immediate and bloody blow from the full force of Scarlett's claws but, gritting my teeth rather than withdrawing my wounded hand, I wedged it farther into their struggle until I had Homer firmly by the scruff of his neck.

Truth be told, I was angrier at Homer in that moment than I was at Scarlett—angrier at him than I'd ever been at any point in all our life together. I knew to a certainty that this fight was mostly, if not entirely, Homer's doing. Scarlett—who religiously avoided close physical contact with Homer even on a good day—would have tried to get away from him long before things had escalated to this point. If she hadn't done so, it could only be because Homer hadn't let her. That her usual round of claws-out warning slaps hadn't deterred him, and her far-superior weight hadn't overpowered him and guaranteed her escape at the outset, was a testament to how riled Homer must have been before the actual, serious fight had even started.

So I was towering in my fury as I lifted Homer off Scarlett by the nape of his neck. (*How could you do this?! How could you do this NOW, when we're still mourning Vashti?!*) And Homer was furious at me right back. I still don't know how he managed it, with the fur of his neck clenched so tightly in my fist, but he turned his head around—pulling so hard against my grip that the skin of his face stretched back until his teeth were fully bared in a violent grimace—and sank those teeth deep into my hand. He bit me *hard*. His canines struck a nerve in the tender flesh of my palm, and a white-hot bolt of pain shot all the way up my arm.

I dropped Homer instantly and sank to the floor, clutching my injured hand and letting fly a high-volume string of obscenities in both English and Spanish that I won't embarrass myself by repeating here (although they must have given our neighbors rather a turn). Scarlett flew from the living room and down the bedroom hallway, into the guest room at the far end of the apartment—fleeing me, no doubt, as much as she was fleeing Homer.

Homer had rarely ever hurt me before, and had never done so intentionally. Usually, hearing me cry out in pain was enough to bring on instant contrition and a round of apologetic head-bonks.

Standing on the floor facing me now, the fur of his back and tail puffed out as far as it would go, Homer hesitated for a moment, as if wavering between his current rage and the force of habits built up over the previous thirteen years. Then, hissing wildly at me, at the retreating Scarlett, at the heavens themselves, he turned and ran for the master bedroom and burrowed deep under the bed—finally managing, after years of trying, to hide successfully. I was reminded of myself at thirteen, when—positive that I was the first and only teenager ever to be so thoroughly misunderstood by her parents—I'd storm down the hallway to my bedroom after an argument, slamming the door behind me.

Our apartment was almost preternaturally quiet over the next couple of hours. Scarlett and Homer made brief, tentative appearances in the living room eventually, as if testing the waters, studiously avoiding each other and me before heading once again for the solitude of their respective bedroom sanctuaries. Though I didn't see much of them, I saw enough to ascertain that neither cat was bleeding or limping, or swelling up in an ear or limb.

I, however, hadn't fared as well. By the time Laurence arrived home, my right hand had swollen to roughly the size of a catcher's mitt. Aghast, he immediately ferried me to the emergency room for a tetanus shot and antibiotics.

When you spend five or six hours in the emergency room (*My cat bit me*, in the realm of ER triage, not carrying quite the same urgency as *I'm having a heart attack* or *I've been shot*) you have plenty of time to think. I was long past being angry at Homer by then. After all, I had Laurence and my family—and the entirety of the cat-loving internet—to console me in my grief over Vashti. But who did Homer have?

I had made a half-hearted effort to be supportive, to help my cats through whatever grief they might be feeling. Clearly, however, I had drastically underestimated their needs. The intensity of Homer's pain and anger—because who among us is ever *not* angry when someone we love leaves us behind?—was proof. When you got right down to it, I had nobody to blame for that interminable wait in the ER—and the bruising tetanus shot that followed—but myself.

🐾 🐾

I HAD TAKEN VASHTI's name from the story of the Jewish holiday known as Purim. The story begins when the proud and beautiful Queen Vashti, first among the wives of the king of Persia, is exiled from the land for refusing to dance naked at the command of her husband. The king then sends out an order to round up all the most beautiful young virgins in Persia so that he might choose a replacement queen. Among the lovely women paraded before the king's discriminating eye, the loveliest of all is a young Jewish girl named Esther, who is duly elevated to the exalted position of queen in a move that would eventually prove fateful for Persian Jews.

With *our* Vashti gone—along with Homer's happy-go-lucky toy worm—and in the wake of that ugly fight between Scarlett and Homer, I conducted my own beauty pageant of sorts. Instead of gathering a coterie of Persian virgins, however, I scoured the Internet—and every pet supplies store within a reasonable traveling radius of our apartment—for cat toys, hoping that one among them might be sufficient to bring some joy back into Homer's heart.

My first thought was to try to find a brand-new version of the exact same worm, which had been one of dozens of identical toy worms on the shelf when I'd bought it in Miami more than fifteen years ago. I didn't remember it having cost much more than a dollar, and surely such an inexpensive and unremarkable plaything—just three little yarn balls with a bell at one end—must still exist.

So, it was with profound frustration and disappointment that, after searching high and low, I had to accept that I was searching in vain. I looked through page after page of cat toys online, browsing both large retailers like Amazon and Walmart and also small mom-and-pop shops with mail-order businesses in far-flung places like Idaho and New Mexico. I walked or took trains and buses to a full complement of Manhattan's pet supply retailers, hitting every single PetSmart in the city and also taking in my purview as many local stores as I could find: Litter and Leashes only three blocks from my home; Petopia, a legendary cornucopia of organic pet care options, in the East Village; Spoiled Brats in Hell's Kitchen; Happy Feet in Midtown; Pet Central in Murray Hill; Petropolis way down in the Financial District. I even traveled to the Upper East Side to try Pet Town in Yorkville. Time after time, I drew amateurish sketches of the worm on the backs of receipts and other scraps of paper I found in my purse, trying to describe to a veritable army of happy-to-help sales clerks exactly what I was looking for.

In return I was shown just about every kind of toy worm imaginable—worms made from felt and plastic and rubber and gel and pipe cleaners; monochromatic worms and worms in vibrant rainbow hues; worms that were faceless and worms that bore ecstatic, manic-eyed grins; worms with neon stripes and wildly colored tufts of hair, like Troll dolls, atop their heads. I was also presented with anything that might, if you squinted, potentially be considered worm-*ish*, like toy snakes and centipedes. Sometimes a sales clerk would even haul out the *Yeowww!* brand of catnip-filled cloth cigars—which, while bearing an undeniably Freudian resemblance to the toy I sought, weren't quite the thing. Sometimes a cigar is just a cigar, but it's almost never a worm.

It was probably just as well that I couldn't find what I was looking for—because even if I had, my quest was doomed from the outset. What difference would it have made if I'd found something that looked exactly like the playmate Homer had lost? Homer didn't know what things *looked* like. He knew only how things smelled, how they felt in his paws or against the fur of his face. A new toy worm would never come to him pre-manhandled by Scarlett and Vashti. Fresh from the pet store, it wouldn't carry the scent of the family he'd been adopted into, the big sisters to whom he'd pledged his heart from his very first day with us—an aroma that told him *You are home* even when he was in some new house in a different city where everything but his family and his inanimate best friend was strange and unsettling.

I didn't want to come home from these forays empty-handed, however. From one shopping bag after another I pulled a seemingly endless array of brand-new toys featuring balls, bells, feathers, tails, and catnip. Trying to engage Homer's interest in them—to tempt him back into being his old, playful self—reminded me of my earliest days trying to win over Scarlett as a kitten. "What's *this*, Homer?" I'd say in that same playful, faux-astonished, talking-to-a-cat voice as I dangled one toy after another enticingly over his head. "What's *this*?"

Homer was far more willing to indulge me now than Scarlett had been then, giving each and every bauble I offered at least a few minutes of his attention. And while there was no specific toy that he seemed to take to more than the others, he showed a decided preference for anything stuffed with catnip. I had high hopes for one that was basically just a big round cloth ball, filled nearly to bursting with 'nip. Homer's undivided interest in the catnip ball lasted for two whole days, during which I thrilled with optimism as I watched him lovingly hug it to his chest with his front legs and kick "bunny feet" at it with his hind ones. But then, one morning, I came into the living room to find that he had systematically gnawed away at the cloth ball's stitching to spill the catnip it contained into an enormous mound on the floor—which he then proceeded to mush his whole face into. When he lifted his 'nip-covered snout to acknowledge my entrance, he looked not unlike Al Pacino in the final scenes of *Scarface*.

(A tip for cat parents: If you don't talk to your cats about 'nip, who will?)

Scarlett herself would often come out to investigate these proceedings. The expression on her face, as she found me doing my best to coax some enthusiasm from Homer with one toy after another, struck me as unmistakably amused. *I see we're doing this again...*

There had been no fresh outbreaks of violence since that one terrible afternoon, although Scarlett and Homer now regarded each other with a certain overly polite wariness. So I was more than a little surprised to find that, sometimes, it seemed almost as if Scarlett was allowing Homer to play with her—or, at least, tolerating his overtures toward play more indulgently than she'd ever done in the past. If, after batting a belled ball lazily a couple of times between her paws, she then took a few running steps after it as it rolled away and Homer ran after her, she didn't immediately turn on him with a snarl (*Stop crowding me!*) and walk off in a huff. Or if she was nuzzling a new catnip toy and Homer muscled his way in on the action, curious to know what she was so interested in, she stepped aside quietly without even whacking him in the face—although, once she'd allowed Homer a few exploratory sniffs, she'd use her shoulder to push him out of the way and reclaim the toy for herself.

Perhaps she'd been cowed by that thunderous and wholly unprecedented display of Homer's temper—one previously only hinted at during vet visits but never displayed in front of the other cats. But I don't think so. Her expression and posture didn't appear fearful. Rather, she seemed—dare I say it?—almost patient with Homer. Almost as if she had picked up some of Vashti's characteristic gentleness, after all these years. Or maybe it was just that, suddenly finding herself as short on friends as Homer was—and heading irreversibly toward old age herself—she'd come to appreciate the value of having a companion. Self-possessed in her crusty aloofness as Scarlett always was, it was difficult to tell what effect, if any, Vashti's loss had had on her. But perhaps she'd decided that wanting to be alone most of the time wasn't quite the same thing as *having* to be alone *all* of the time.

Then one evening, Laurence and I arrived home to a scene I'd never thought I'd live to see: In the middle of the living room rug—in the middle of a colorful clutter of new, barely used cat toys—Scarlett and Homer were curled up together, locked chest to chest and face to face, each with one leg slung over the other's back, holding each other in a full body embrace as they napped soundly and peacefully.

If I'd seen an actual miracle take place before my eyes—the Red Sea parting, manna raining from the heavens, my uncle Sasha picking up a check—I couldn't have been more flabbergasted.

I was torn between wanting to stand there and watch them, and wanting to beat a hasty retreat before one or both of them sensed my presence and the spell was broken. Silently waving Laurence into the living room behind me, with a warning finger raised to my lips, I bent down to slip off my shoes and tiptoed through the living room toward our bedroom. I motioned to Laurence that he should do the same.

"Did you put something in their water?" he whispered to me.

"Shhhh," I whispered back. "You'll ruin the moment."

I SUSPECT THAT, IN my mad hunt for a new toy that Homer would love just as much as he'd loved the old one, I'd been engaging in a bit of magical thinking. Deep down, I had the wholly irrational idea that if I could get Homer to act young again, he would actually *be* young again. And if Homer were young again, maybe I would be too—maybe all of us would. Maybe we could turn back the clock far enough even to have my Vashti-girl—in some way, and against all reason—with us once more. Or, at the very least, maybe it would feel that way. Maybe our home would feel like it used to, falling into the same familiar rhythms we'd known so well and for so long that the routines of our days and our interactions with each other had relied almost more on muscle memory than actual thought.

But that was never in the cards. Clocks weren't going to turn back, Vashti would never return, and no new toy worm—or toy of any kind—was going to replace the one that Homer had loved. Just like the new cats who would eventually come into our lives were never going to replace Vashti. You can't replace something you've loved and lost—which isn't to say that you can't love again.

Homer and Scarlett never quite became the best and closest friends that Homer had always imagined—or wished—they were. Scarlett still preferred spending most of her time alone, or alone with me. But the two of them would now cuddle up together from time to time, which was a genuinely shocking breakthrough in the annals of Scarlett's personal history. And Homer also got more comfortable spending time in rooms by himself if I wasn't around and Scarlett wouldn't let him get too close—which, after so many years of having his happiness in life solely invested in the physical presence of others, was probably a healthy development.

Life in a family is a series of ever-shifting connections, the complexity of which we tend to overlook because on the surface everything seems so simple and straightforward—everyone has their assigned role (parent, spouse, sibling) and tends to go through the everyday motions of that role without too much conscious thought. A family is like a body in that way, an amalgam of constituent parts (arms, legs, neck) that each work separately but still, together, create a whole. And when a wound opens, the body closes over the rupture. The resulting scar tissue may not look the same, but sometimes it ends up being even stronger.

So it was for us after Vashti was gone. It was time itself, and not some ersatz "replacement," that eventually mended the breach.

The day came, nearly two years later, when Homer was the only cat left—believing to the last that he and Scarlett had loved each other more than anyone ever had, except for him and me. And this, finally, was too much loneliness to expect a cat as social as Homer to simply work through and move past on his own—no matter how much time we might have given him. So we adopted a coal-black, roly-poly, "tripod" kitten we named Clayton, along with his littermate, a sleekly gorgeous black beauty we called Fanny.

If Scarlett had seemed, in the wake of Vashti's passing, to take on a little bit of Vashti's personality, it was amusing now to see Homer occasionally breaking out his Scarlett impression when tasked, for the very first time, with being the "big cat" of the house. Clayton hero-worshipped Homer right from the first, fascinated with every little thing Homer did and refusing to leave his side for even a minute if he could help it. Sometimes—when Homer was finally tired of being followed, ogled, inspected, and interfered with, and his patience wore thin—I smiled to see him raise one warning paw, just as Scarlett used to, and whap Clayton in the face a few times.

Clayton never seemed to take this too personally, continuing to bounce excitedly after Homer as he walked from room to room or jumped on and off the bed or couch or countertops—forever uttering his trademark, "*MEEEEEEEEE!*" In my head, I always saw them as Spike the Bulldog and Chester the Terrier from those old Looney Tunes cartoons—Homer striding impressively down the hallway while Clayton scampered eagerly around him in circles. *What are you doing, Homer? What are you doing today? Where are you going, Homer? Huh? Can I come with you, Homer? Can I?*—until finally Homer's paw would rise to backhand Clayton's snout with an impatient, *Ehhhhh . . . shut up.*

For all his newfound curmudgeonliness, it turned out that Clayton and Fanny made for better playmates than the fake worm ever had, and Homer soon warmed up to their naked adoration of him. His last years were as filled with playfulness, roughhousing, and adventure games as his first had been—maybe even more so.

What I learned is that while clocks will never run backward, and things that are lost may never return, the heart is a resilient organ that knows how to take care of itself—if you get out of its way and allow it to do so.

I also learned that, if you've just lost someone you loved dearly, and your world has flipped over into some Bizarro version of itself that makes you feel like a stranger in your own life, you should never—under any circumstances—in the freshness of your grief listen to "Landslide" by Fleetwood Mac.

Seriously. Don't do it.

THE HILARIOUS FIRST INSTALLMENT IN THE "PAWSOME" SERIES!

PAWSOME!
HEAD BONKS, RASPY TONGUES, AND 101 REASONS WHY CATS MAKE US SO, SO HAPPY

GWEN COOPER
NEW YORK TIMES BESTSELLING AUTHOR OF HOMER'S ODYSSEY

"Gwen has an astute ability to describe being a cat person in a truthful and humorous way that entertains and keeps you coming back. I actually read this twice!"
--Amazon Reviewer

———— ✳ ————

The *purrfect* treat for the cat lover in your life--or for yourself!

About the Author

GWEN COOPER IS THE *New York Times* bestselling author of the memoirs *Homer's Odyssey: A Fearless Feline Tale, or How I Learned About Love and Life with a Blind Wonder Cat*; *Homer: The Ninth Life of a Blind Wonder Cat*; and *My Life in a Cat House: True Tales of Love, Laughter, and Living with Five Felines*, as well as the novel *Love Saves the Day*, narrated from a rescue cat's point of view. Her work has been published in more than two-dozen languages. She is a frequent speaker at shelter fundraisers and donates 10% of her royalties from *Homer's Odyssey* to organizations that serve abused, abandoned, and disabled animals.

Gwen lives in New Jersey with her husband, Laurence. She also lives with her two perfect cats—Clayton "the Tripod" and his litter-mate, Fanny—who aren't impressed with any of it.

Get a FREE copy of an all-new book about Homer and the gang!
Visit www.gwencooper.com